Rocks and Minerals

Connecting Students to Science Series

By
LAVERNE LOGAN

COPYRIGHT © 2002 Mark Twain Media, Inc.

ISBN 1-58037-219-8

Printing No. CD-1565

Mark Twain Media, Inc., Publishers
Distributed by Carson-Dellosa Publishing Company, Inc.

Table of Contents

Introduction to the Series

The Connecting Students to Science Series is designed for grades 5–8. The series introduces the following topics: Simple Machines, Electricity and Magnetism, Rocks and Minerals, Atmosphere and Weather, Chemistry, Light and Color, Sound, and The Solar System. Each book contains an introduction to the topic, naive concepts, inquiry activities, content integration, children's literature connections, curriculum resources, assessment documents, materials lists, and a bibliography.

Students will develop an understanding of the concepts and processes of science through the use of good scientific techniques. Students will be engaged in higher-level thinking skills while doing fun and interesting activities. All of the activities are aligned with the National Science Education Standards and National Council of Teachers of Mathematics Standards.

This series is written for classroom teachers, parents, families, and students. The books in this series can be used as a full unit of study or as individual lessons to supplement existing textbooks or curriculum programs. Activities are designed to be pedagogically sound, hands-on, minds-on science activities that support the National Science Education Standards (NSES). Parents and students could use this series as an enhancement to what is being done in the classroom or as a tutorial at home. The procedures and content background are clearly explained in the introduction and within the individual activities. Materials used in the activities are commonly found in classrooms and homes.

Introduction to the Topic and Major Concepts

This curricular resource is designed to capitalize on students' natural interest in the world around them. Rocks and minerals are a very real part of students' everyday lives. Rocks and minerals provide resources for many of the goods and related services students enjoy daily. In the activities to follow, students will investigate the composition of the earth; the relationship between rocks and minerals; the many uses of minerals by humankind; mineral identification; families and formation of igneous, metamorphic, and sedimentary rocks; rock formation within the rock cycle; physical properties and formation of sand; fossils; and an individual inquiry question(s).

The study of rocks and minerals provides an excellent opportunity for hands-on, minds-on investigations that utilize many of the science process skills. Students will apply inference skills and both direct and indirect observation as they analyze the findings of the activities. To aid in maintaining a balance between process and content, two performance-based, formative assessment devices appear throughout each activity. The initial introductory activity includes the construction of a **K**now—**W**ant to Know—**L**earned chart. The chart is revisited and main-

tained at the conclusion of each activity, as naive conceptions are altered, new questions arise, and new information is learned. In the first lesson, students create three-dimensional Earth models and an accompanying poster, to which they add information throughout each activity. The intent of the model is to preserve and represent the concepts in a three-dimensional format.

The Procedures section of each activity is directed toward the teacher or parent as a guide to setting up the activity. The Summary section is also a teacher/parent section that can be used to determine how well the student has mastered the concepts.

Space for student free response is provided in the Exploration/Data Collection and Discussion Questions/Assessment sections; however, individual science journals/logs may be readily substituted.

As with any effective teaching tool, you are urged to modify and adapt any of the activities in this book to best suit the individual needs of your students. Best wishes as you enjoy the wonderful world of rocks and minerals!

Naive Concepts and Terminology Definitions

Introduction

Our understanding of the natural world is directly related to commonly occurring experiences, including those that occur in and out of the science classroom. Sometimes the everyday descriptions of phenomena lead to concepts that are either incomplete or inaccurate. For example, students may observe a glass of iced tea with water collecting and running down the outside of the glass and state, "The glass is sweating." Such a statement may lead us to inaccurately infer as to the source of the moisture on the outside of the glass. A careful and thoughtful analysis of this phenomena might lead us to infer that the moisture on the outside of the glass is condensation and that the source of the moisture is the water vapor from the surrounding air.

We may refer to our developing conception of the world and the way things work or the way life works as being in the process of development. In this way, some of our ideas may be naive. Some authors refer to these developing concepts as misconceptions. For the purpose of this resource, we will refer to them as naive ideas.

Some naive ideas related to rocks and minerals

One area for potential naive conceptions is related to the terminology used. Many commonly used words have a specific and alternative meaning in science. A second area that may serve as a source for naive conceptions occurs when intuitive ideas gained through everyday experience are contrary to the more formal structure of scientific concepts.

Words that may serve as a source of confusion include:

- **asthenosphere** - the upper portion of the mantle; molten rock with plastic-like qualities upon which the lithospheric plates move.

- **core** - innermost portion of the earth; divided into a solid, inner core and a dense, liquid, outer core.

- **convection currents** - movements in fluids caused by heat; students may not attribute movements of the earth's plates to heat and convection.

- **convergent plate boundaries** - a line along which diverging plates collide.

- **crust** - a more common term for the outermost portion of the earth; see also lithosphere.

- **divergent plate boundaries** - a line along which diverging plates move away from each other; also known as sea-floor spreading; students may mistakenly assume volcanoes only occur above sea-level.

- **gemstone** - nonmetallic minerals known for their attractive colors.

Naive Concepts and Terminology Definitions (cont.)

- **hardness** - a common test for the identification of minerals; relative to indexed minerals on the Mohs' scale.

- **igneous rock** - rocks that are formed by the crystallization of magma.

- **lava** - molten rock that has been extruded through the surface of the earth; students may confuse lava with magma.

- **lithosphere** - the thin, outer, crustal layer of the earth; students may think of spheres only in relation to the atmosphere, e.g., what is above the earth.

- **lithification** - the process of compaction and cementation of rock particles to form layered rocks; catalyst for the formation of sedimentary rocks.

- **luster** - the reaction of the surface of a mineral to light.

- **magma** - molten rock that is located beneath the surface of the earth; students may confuse magma with lava.

- **mantle** - 1,800-mile-thick molten layer, directly beneath the thin crust of the earth; students may assume the earth is solid to the core.

- **metamorphic rock** - rocks that are formed by chemical alteration of previously existing rocks, due to heat and pressure.

- **mineral** - a solid, inorganic crystalline substance with a definite chemical composition; students may assume that rocks and minerals are interchangeable.

- **Mohs' scale** - an index of minerals of varying hardness.

- **ore** - minerals that are economically viable to extract.

- **plate tectonics** - the currently accepted theory of the movement of the earth's plates across the asthenosphere; students may not believe the earth's crust moves.

- **sedimentary rock** - rocks that are formed by the layering of sediments due to erosion and weathering of existing rocks and organic material.

- **silicon-oxygen tetrahedron** - the basic building block of rock-forming minerals.

- **weathering** - a change in the physical and/or chemical composition of a rock due to the forces of nature.

National Standards

National Science Education Standards (NSES) NRC, 1996

National Research Council (1996). *National Science Education Standards.* Washington, D.C.: National Academy Press.

Unifying Concepts: K-12

Systems, Order, and Organization - The natural and designed world is complex. Scientists and students learn to define small portions for the convenience of investigation. The units of investigation can be referred to as systems. A system is an organized group of related objects or components that form a whole. Systems can consist of machines.

Systems, Order, and Organization
The goal of this standard is to …
• Think and analyze in terms of systems.
• Assume that the behavior of the universe is not capricious. Nature is predictable.
• Understand the regularities in a system.
• Understand that prediction is the use of knowledge to identify and explain observations.
• Understand that the behavior of matter, objects, organisms, or events has order and can be described statistically.

Evidence, Models, and Explanation
The goal of this standard is to …
• Recognize that the evidence consists of observations and data on which to base scientific explanations.
• Recognize that models have explanatory power.
• Recognize that scientific explanations incorporate existing scientific knowledge (laws, principles, theories, paradigms, models) and new evidence from observations, experiments, or models.
• Recognize that scientific explanations should reflect a rich scientific knowledge base, evidence of logic, higher levels of analysis, greater tolerance of criticism and uncertainty, and a clear demonstration of the relationship between logic, evidence, and current knowledge.

Change, Constancy, and Measurement
The goal of this standard is to …
• Recognize that some properties of objects are characterized by constancy, including the speed of light, the charge of an electron, and the total mass plus energy of the universe.
• Recognize that changes might occur in the properties of materials, the position of objects, motion, and the form and function of systems.
• Recognize that changes in systems can be quantified.
• Recognize that measurement systems may be used to clarify observations.

National Standards (cont.)

Form and Function

The goal of this standard is to …
- Recognize that the form of an object is frequently related to its use, operation, or function.
- Recognize that function frequently relies on form.
- Recognize that form and function apply to different levels of organization.
- Enable students to explain function by referring to form and explain form by referring to function.

NSES Content Standard A: Inquiry
- Abilities necessary to do scientific inquiry
  * Identify questions that can be answered through scientific investigations.
  * Design and conduct a scientific investigation.
  * Use appropriate tools and techniques to gather, analyze, and interpret data.
  * Develop descriptions, explanations, predictions, and models using evidence.
  * Think critically and logically to make relationships between evidence and explanations.
  * Recognize and analyze alternative explanations and predictions.
  * Communicate scientific procedures and explanations.
  * Use mathematics in all aspects of scientific inquiry.
- Understanding about inquiry
  * Different kinds of questions suggest different kinds of scientific investigations.
  * Current scientific knowledge and understanding guide scientific investigations.
  * Mathematics is important in all aspects of scientific inquiry.
  * Technology used to gather data enhances accuracy and allows scientists to analyze and quantify the results of investigations.
  * Scientific explanations emphasize evidence, have logically consistent arguments, and use scientific principles, models, and theories.
  * Science advances through legitimate skepticism.
  * Scientific investigations sometimes result in new ideas and phenomena for study, generate new methods or procedures, or develop new technologies to improve data collection.

NSES Content Standard B: Properties and Changes of Properties in Matter 5-8

NSES Content Standard D: Structure of the Earth System 5-8

NSES Content Standard D: Earth in the Solar System 5-8

NSES Content Standard E: Science and Technology 5-8
- Abilities of technological design
  * Identify appropriate problems for technological design.
  * Design a solution or product.
  * Implement the proposed design.

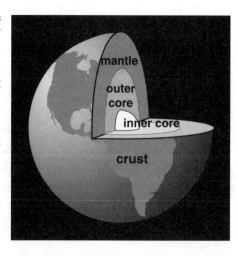

National Standards (cont.)

* Evaluate completed technological designs or products.
* Communicate the process of technological design.
• Understanding about science and technology
    * Scientific inquiry and technological design have similarities and differences.
    * Many people in different cultures have made and continue to make contributions.
    * Science and technology are reciprocal.
    * Perfectly designed solutions do not exist.
    * Technological designs have constraints.
    * Technological solutions have intended benefits and unintended consequences.

NSES Content Standard F: Science in Personal and Social Perspectives 5-8
• Science and technology in society
    * Science influences society through its knowledge and world view.
    * Societal challenges often inspire questions for scientific research.
    * Technology influences society through its products and processes.
    * Scientists and engineers work in many different settings.
    * Science cannot answer all questions, and technology cannot solve all human problems.

NSES Content Standard G: History and Nature of Science 5-8
• Science as human endeavor
• Nature of science
    * Scientists formulate and test their explanations of nature using observation, experiments, and theoretical and mathematical models.
    * It is normal for scientists to differ with one another about interpretation of evidence and theory.
    * It is part of scientific inquiry for scientists to evaluate the results of other scientists' work.
• History of science
    * Many individuals have contributed to the traditions of science.
    * Science has been and is practiced by different individuals in different cultures.
    * Tracing the history of science can show how difficult it was for scientific innovators to break through the accepted ideas of their time to reach the conclusions we now accept.

National Standards (cont.)

Standards for Technological Literacy (STL) ITEA, 2000

International Technology Education Association (2000). *Standards for Technological Literacy.* Reston, VA: International Technology Education Association.

The Nature of Technology
Students will develop an understanding of the:
1. Characteristics and scope of technology.
2. Core concepts of technology.
3. Relationships among technologies and the connections between technology and other fields of study.

Technology and Society
Students will develop an understanding of the:
4. Cultural, social, economic, and political effects of technology.
5. Effects of technology on the environment.
6. Role of society in the development and use of technology.
7. Influence of technology on history.

Design
Students will develop an understanding of the:
8. Attributes of design.
9. Engineering design.
10. Role of troubleshooting, research and development, invention and innovation, and experimentation in problem solving.

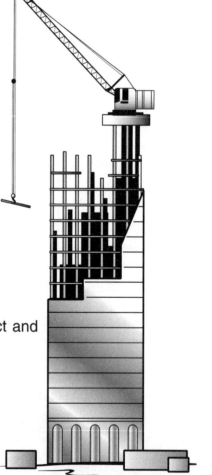

Abilities for a Technological World
Students will develop the abilities to:
11. Apply the design process.
12. Use and maintain technological products and systems.
13. Assess the impact of products and systems.

The Designed World
Students will develop an understanding of and be able to select and use:
14. Medical technologies.
15. Agricultural and related biotechnologies.
16. Energy and power technologies.
17. Information and communication technologies.
18. Transportation technologies.
19. Manufacturing technologies.
20. Construction technologies.

National Standards (cont.)

Principles and Standards for School Mathematics (NCTM), 2000

National Council for Teachers of Mathematics (2000). *Principles and Standards for School Mathematics.* Reston, VA: National Council for Teachers of Mathematics.

Number and Operations
Students will be enabled to:
- Understand numbers, ways of representing numbers, relationships among numbers, and number systems.
- Understand meanings of operations and how they relate to one another.
- Compute fluently and make reasonable estimates.

Algebra
Students will be enabled to:
- Understand patterns, relations, and functions.
- Represent and analyze mathematical situations and structures using algebraic symbols.
- Use mathematical models to represent and understand quantitative relationships.
- Analyze change in various contexts.

Geometry
Students will be enabled to:
- Analyze characteristics and properties of two- and three-dimensional geometric shapes and develop mathematical arguments about geometric relationships.
- Specify locations and describe spatial relationships using coordinate geometry and other representational systems.
- Apply transformations and use symmetry to analyze mathematical situations.
- Use visualization, spatial reasoning, and geometric modeling to solve problems.

Measurement
Students will be enabled to:
- Understand measurable attributes of objects and the units, systems, and processes of measurement.
- Apply appropriate techniques, tools, and formulas to determine measurements.

Data Analysis and Probability
Students will be enabled to:
- Formulate questions that can be addressed with data and collect, organize, and display relevant data to answer them.
- Select and use appropriate statistical methods to analyze data.
- Develop and evaluate inferences and predictions that are based on data.
- Understand and apply basic concepts of probability.

Science Process Skills

Introduction: Science is organized curiosity, and important parts of this organization are the thinking skills or information-processing skills. We ask the question "Why?" and then must plan a strategy for answering. In the process of answering our questions, we make and carefully record observations, make predictions, identify and control variables, measure, make inferences, and communicate our findings. Additional skills may be called upon, depending on the nature of our questions. In this way, science is a verb involving the active manipulation of materials and careful thinking. Science is dependent on language, math, and reading skills, as well as the specialized thinking skills associated with identifying and solving problems.

BASIC PROCESS SKILLS

Classifying: Grouping, ordering, arranging, or distributing objects, events, or information into categories based on properties or criteria, according to some method or system.

> Example: Classifying rocks and minerals, e.g., three major classifications of rocks and their families.

Observing: Using the senses (or extensions of the senses) to gather information about an object or event.

> Example: Observing physical properties of rocks and minerals; critical for compare and contrast skills, which are needed for analysis.

Measuring: Using both standard and nonstandard measures or estimates to describe the dimensions of an object or event. Making quantitative observations.

> Example: Measuring the density of minerals.

Inferring: Making an interpretation or conclusion based on reasoning to explain an observation.

> Example: Stating the types of life and living conditions from fossil evidence.

Communicating: Communicating ideas through speaking or writing. Students may share the results of investigations, collaborate on solving problems, and gather and interpret data both orally and in writing. Using graphs, charts, and diagrams to describe data.

> Example: Describing an event or a set of observations. Participating in brainstorming and hypothesizing before an investigation. Formulating initial and follow-up questions in the study of a topic. Summarizing data, interpreting findings, and offering conclusions. Questioning or refuting previous findings.

Science Process Skills (cont.)

Predicting: Making a forecast of future events or conditions in the context of previous observations and experiences.

> Example: Stating, "Magma containing high levels of silica will cause volcanoes to explode more violently."

Manipulating Materials: Handling or treating materials and equipment skillfully and effectively.

> Example: Using a rock hammer, hand lens, and sieves to analyze rock samples.

Using Numbers: Applying mathematical rules or formulas to calculate quantities or determine relationships from basic measurements.

> Example: Determining the relative thickness of the layers of the earth.

Developing Vocabulary: Specialized terminology and unique uses of common words in relation to a given topic need to be identified and given meaning.

> Example: Using context clues, working definitions, glossaries or dictionaries, word structure (roots, prefixes, suffixes), and synonyms and antonyms to clarify meaning, i.e., sedimentary, metamorphic, and igneous rocks; minerals; Mohs' scale; ore; mantle; core; lithosphere; plate tectonics; convergent plate boundaries; divergent plate boundaries.

Questioning: Questions serve to focus inquiry, determine prior knowledge, and establish purposes or expectations for an investigation. An active search for information is promoted when questions are used.

> Example: Using what is already known about a topic or concept to formulate questions for further investigation; hypothesizing and predicting prior to gathering data; or formulating questions as new information is acquired.

Using Clues: Key words and symbols convey significant meaning in messages. Organizational patterns facilitate comprehension of major ideas. Graphic features clarify textual information.

> Example: Listing or underlining words and phrases that carry the most important details, or relating key words together to express a main idea or concept.

Science Process Skills (cont.)

INTEGRATED PROCESS SKILLS

Creating Models: Displaying information by means of graphic illustrations or other multisensory representations.

> Example: Drawing a graph or diagram; constructing a three-dimensional object, e.g., Earth model; using a digital camera to record an event; constructing a chart or table; or producing a picture or map that illustrates information about the earth and its geologic features.

Formulating Hypotheses: Stating or constructing a statement that is testable about what is thought to be the expected outcome of an experiment (based on reasoning).

> Example: Making a statement to be used as the basis for an experiment: "If the substance is a combination of minerals, it must be some sort of rock."

Generalizing: Drawing general conclusions from particulars.

> Example: Making a summary statement following analysis of experimental results: "The fossil evidence and layers of this rock indicate that it is some sort of sedimentary rock."

Identifying and Controlling Variables: Recognizing the characteristics of objects or factors in events that are constant or change under different conditions and that can affect an experimental outcome, keeping most variables constant while manipulating only one variable.

> Example: Controlling variables in an experiment to determine the viscosity of substances representing magmas.

Defining Operationally: Stating how to measure a variable in an experiment; defining a variable according to the actions or operations to be performed on or with it.

> Example: Defining minerals as solid, inorganic crystalline substances with definite chemical compositions.

Recording and Interpreting Data: Collecting bits of information about objects and events that illustrate a specific situation, organizing and analyzing data that has been obtained, and drawing conclusions from it by determining apparent patterns or relationships in the data.

> Example: Recording data (taking notes, making lists/outlines, recording numbers on charts/graphs, making tape recordings, taking photographs, writing numbers of results of observations/measurements) from observations to determine the physical properties of rocks and minerals.

Science Process Skills (cont.)

Making Decisions: Identifying alternatives and choosing a course of action from among alternatives after basing the judgment for the selection on justifiable reasons.

> Example: Determining optimum location(s) for rocks and minerals collecting.

Experimenting: Being able to conduct an experiment, including asking an appropriate question, stating a hypothesis, identifying and controlling variables, operationally defining those variables, designing a "fair" experiment, and interpreting the results of an experiment.

> Example: Formulating a researchable question, identifying and controlling variables including a manipulated and responding variable, data collection, data analysis, drawing conclusions, and formulating new questions as a result of the conclusions.

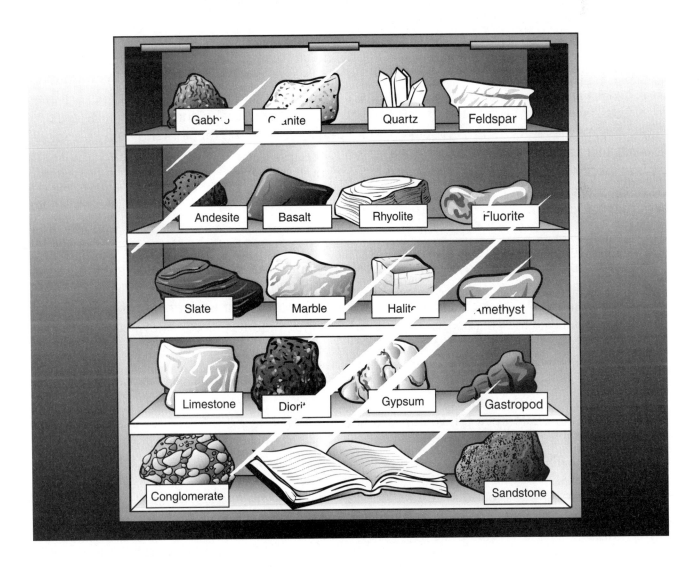

Name: _____ Date: _____

Introductory Activity: K-W-L Rocks and Minerals

What Do We Know About Rocks and Minerals?

1. As a preliminary activity, construct a large K-W-L chart as a class. A flip chart or a large piece of freezer paper or poster board placed on a bulletin board or wall may be used. An example is shown below.

Know	Want to Know	Learned

2. Lead a class discussion to discover students' current understanding of rocks and minerals. List student beliefs under the "Know" column. Stress that this is what we believe to be the case, at this point in time. Point out that this information might change as we discover more information via the activities to come.

3. The ideas provided by the students can provide valuable insight, which provides the basis for many instructional decisions. Students are likely to hold naive conceptions regarding rocks and minerals; this column is where the naive conceptions will appear. This will provide a visual representation of what students think about rocks and minerals. Be sure to list all of the ideas as written/spoken by students, despite the fact that they may be scientifically inaccurate or incomplete. As an ongoing formative assessment, return to this list as opportunities to correct naive conceptions occur.

What Questions Do We Have About Rocks and Minerals?

1. Within the spirit of scientific inquiry, it is wise to consider student-generated questions for investigation. This can be done individually, in small groups, or as a class. Near the end of the book, students are provided with an opportunity to plan and conduct individual inquiry investigations. As a result, it is recommended to generate a preliminary list of questions as a class. As with the section that describes what the students already know, questions may be added as the activities are completed. This mirrors the process of science, e.g., new information often yields new questions for further research.

2. Some sample questions students may have include:
   • What is the difference between rocks and minerals?
   • Are gold and silver minerals?
   • How do minerals compare with the types of minerals commonly associated with vitamins?
   • Why are minerals found in certain locations of the earth and not others?
   • What are the most common rocks and minerals around our area? Why are they found here?

Name: _____ Date: _____

Introductory Activity: K-W-L Rocks and Minerals (cont.)

- What causes the various colors of rocks and minerals?
- What are gems, and how do they compare to rocks and minerals? What makes a gem, a gem?

3. Questions from this list may provide the basis for individual inquiry investigations, found later in the book.

What Have We Learned About Rocks and Minerals?

1. As conclusions are generated from the activities throughout the book, return and add them to the "Learned" column. Cross-check the "Know" column for any changes that may be appropriate. Be creative in editing the "Know" column. Draw a single line through the blatant naive conceptions, e.g., all rocks are found on the earth's surface. Perhaps correct the naive conception by drawing a connecting line to a better explanation found in the "Learned" column. For example, a statement in the "Know" column, "All rocks come from volcanoes," could be specified to include a description of the rock cycle found in the "Learned" column.

2. Ultimately, the goal of the book and related activities is to increase understanding of rocks and minerals by building a "Learned" column while examining the "Know" column for accuracy and depth of thought. Concurrently, new questions for inquiry that arise as investigations unfold should be considered as well.

Note: The K-W-L chart may be completed and maintained individually if the instructor wishes to track the progress of each student. Another option is to have students complete and maintain an individual K-W-L chart and also contribute to an overall class K-W-L.

Know	Want to Know	Learned
Rocks can be formed by volcanoes.	What is magma?	Magma is molten rock below the earth's surface.

Student Inquiry Activity **1** : The Layers of the Earth

Topic: Composition of the Earth

Introductory Statement:

The earth is made of distinct layers. In these activities, you will learn the names of these layers, their compositions, and relative thicknesses.

> **NSES Content Standard D: Structure of the Earth System**
> The solid earth is layered with a lithosphere; hot, convecting mantle; and dense, metallic core.

Science Skills and Concepts:
- Students will identify the layers of the earth.
- Students will describe physical characteristics of the individual layers of the earth.
- Students will compare and contrast the layers of the earth.
- Students will use a model to demonstrate the layers of the earth, their compositions, and relative thicknesses.

Materials/Safety Concerns:
12-inch Styrofoam™ balls; one per student
markers/crayons/colored pencils
modeling clay
large poster board; one per student
tempera paint: green, blue, brown, red, orange

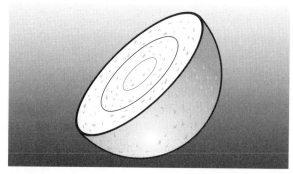

Content Background:

The earth consists of three main layers: crust, mantle, and core. Occasionally, the names of the layers are further refined according to specific location, e.g., inner core, outer core, upper mantle, etc.

The outermost layer of relatively thin **crust** is also called the **lithosphere**. Ranging in thickness from 5 km (3 miles) to 100 km (62 miles), the earth's crust consists of solid, rigid plates. The surface of this layer of the earth is directly observable and accounts for many of the observations students will make during the study of rocks and minerals.

Directly below the lithosphere is the **mantle**, a layer of dense, molten rock ranging from 5 km (3 miles) to 2,900 km (1,802 miles) thick. Almost plastic-like in rigidity, the upper mantle is known as the **asthenosphere**. According to the theory of plate tectonics, the upper mantle provides the basis upon which the earth's plates slide.

The innermost layer of the earth is the **core**. The core consists of two distinct sub-layers, the liquid, outer core with a thickness of 2,270 km (1,411 miles); and the solid, inner core with a thickness of 1,216 km (756 miles).

The layers of the earth are analogous to a layered ball. Many curricular resources cite a hardboiled egg as another analogy. The brittle shell represents the lithosphere; the egg white represents the mantle; and the egg yolk represents the core. As always, models such as an egg

Student Inquiry Activity **1** : The Layers of the Earth (cont.)

should be used with caution so as not to promote naive conceptions, e.g., elliptical shape of egg, solids in all layers, lack of roughly 20 plates on the egg's surface.

Scientists make inferences about the interior of the earth based upon seismic waves. For example, certain seismic waves vary in speed as they travel through liquids and solids. Indirect observations from seismic data allow scientists to infer the composition (liquid or solid) and density of layers of the earth.

Procedures:

This activity will result in the individual construction of a cross-sectional model of the earth and a large poster to accompany the model. As new information is learned in the activities to come, it should be added to the model and poster. The model and poster should be an ongoing performance-based assessment, which should embody the knowledge of rocks and minerals. Specific instructions for additions to the model and poster are included in the activities to come; however, instructors are encouraged to modify the models and posters to meet their students' curriculum needs.

1. Each student should be provided with a 12-inch Styrofoam™ ball and large tagboard poster. Explain to students that although the models and poster will be constructed in this lesson, they will be further developed in upcoming lessons. In addition to the K-W-L charts from the preliminary activity, the models and posters will serve as a repository for new information as it is accrued.

2. Students should measure and lightly mark the balls so they will be able to cut them directly in half, creating two half spheres. Balls can easily be halved using a serrated knife or jigsaw, if available. Caution: Review safety procedures for proper use of a knife and/or cutting device. Teachers may wish to have the balls pre-cut, if safety is a concern.

3. Ask students to speculate how scientists know what is beneath the surface of the earth. Discuss the difference between direct and indirect observations. Ask students to speculate how many layers the earth has and of what substance each is made.

4. Challenge students to research to find the layers of the earth and related information, e.g., thickness, composition, etc. Provide trade books, reference materials, textbooks, and Internet access to aid students in locating the information. Encourage students to be prepared to share their sources of information and compare/contrast their findings with others.

5. Instruct students to illustrate the layers of the earth directly on each half of the balls. At this point, illustrate only the inside (flat) part of the balls. Students should use mathematics to determine the relative thickness of each layer. Layers can be demarcated with a pencil and later colored using markers, crayons, colored pencils, and/or tempera paint. At minimum, students should demark three distinct layers (crust, mantle, and core); some students may include sub-layers, e.g., outer and inner core, upper mantle, etc. All layers and thicknesses should be clearly marked.

Student Inquiry Activity **1** : The Layers of the Earth (cont.)

6. Additional information gleaned about the composition of the earth's interior should be added to the accompanying poster. Cross-references between the model and the poster are encouraged.

7. As students complete the activity, they should compare and contrast their findings with others. Discuss differences and similarities in data collected and reasons why this might be the case.

8. Provide large rubber bands to hold the model halves together (for convenient storage) after construction is completed. Construct a base for the model; cut strips (18 in. x 2 in.) from legal-sized manila folders. Staple the two ends together, forming a collar on which to place the Earth models.

- -

Name: _____ Date: _____

Exploration/Data Collection:

1. Record what you believe to be found underneath the surface of the earth.

_____

_____

_____

_____

_____

_____

_____

2. Extend Question #1 to include "all the way to the center of the earth."

_____

_____

_____

_____

_____

_____

_____

Name: _____ Date: _____

Student Inquiry Activity ▮ : The Layers of the Earth (cont.)

3. Predict the total diameter of the earth, in kilometers. _____

4. Predict the radius of the earth, in kilometers. _____

5. While following instructions from your teacher, convert your findings to a cross-sectional view of the earth in the form of a model (Styrofoam™ ball). Include the following information:
   - at least three distinct layers and
   - the relative thickness of each layer.

   On the poster include the following information:
   - the composition of each layer and
   - a brief summary of how scientists have determined what is inside the earth.

6. Return to Questions #1–4 above and compare your predictions to what you have illustrated and included on the poster. Using a writing instrument of a different color, edit your responses to include more accurate information. Do not erase your original predictions!

7. Compare and contrast your model and poster with at least two other people's. What similarities and differences do you note? What might be the reason for differences?

_____

_____

_____

_____

_____

_____

_____

_____

_____

_____

_____

_____

8. Be sure to cite the sources of your information. You will wish to create a reference sheet for all of the information included on the model and posters, both in this activity and the activities to come.

Name: _____   Date: _____

Student Inquiry Activity ■1■ : The Layers of the Earth (cont.)

Summary/What to Look For:
1. To what extent were students able to articulate the layers of the earth?
2. To what extent were students' predictions accurate?
3. To what extent did students accurately edit their original predictions regarding the layers of the earth?
4. To what extent did students accurately cross-reference the model and poster?
5. To what extent did students describe physical characteristics of the individual layers of the earth?
6. To what extent did students accurately compare and contrast the layers of the earth?

Discussion Questions/Assessment:
1. Critically analyze the statement "I will dig a hole so deep, I will come out in China." What is accurate and inaccurate about this statement?

_____

_____

_____

_____

_____

_____

_____

_____

_____

_____

2. Return to the K-W-L chart. Examine the columns for additions and editing needs based upon what you have learned during these activities, e.g., in what ways has your thinking changed?

Student Inquiry Activity **2** : What's the Difference?

Topic: The Difference Between Rocks and Minerals

Introductory Statement:
Are you aware of the difference between rocks and minerals? These activities are designed for you to discover and clarify the basic difference between rocks and minerals.

NSES Content Standard D: Structure of the Earth System
The solid earth is layered with a lithosphere; hot, convecting mantle; and dense, metallic core.

Science Skills and Concepts:
- Students will define the term *rocks* and provide examples.
- Students will define the term *minerals* and provide examples.
- Students will articulate the difference between rocks and minerals.
- Students will identify physical characteristics/properties of rocks and minerals.

Materials/Safety Concerns:
An assorted selection of mineral samples
Two sandwich bags for each student
Markers
Hand lenses

Content Background:
Minerals are the building blocks for rocks. Minerals are usually elemental compounds in their pure form. Minerals have four common features:
- minerals occur naturally
- minerals are inorganic
- minerals are solids
- minerals have a single chemical composition/structure.

Rocks are mixtures that are usually made up of an assortment of minerals. Occasionally, a rock consists of only mineral, e.g., calcite (limestone). Rock may contain organic materials, e.g., coal. Rocks may have various chemical compositions due to the presence of more than one mineral. Rocks are classified into three main groups: **igneous**, **metamorphic**, and **sedimentary**. These classifications are directly related to processes under which the rocks are formed. Each of these classifications and processes will be investigated in upcoming activities.

Procedures:
1. Many students may not be aware of the difference between rocks and minerals. Urge students to record their current beliefs about the difference between rocks and minerals. Read these responses while watching for evidence of naive conceptions, e.g., there is no difference.

Student Inquiry Activity 2 : What's the Difference? (cont.)

2. Distribute two sandwich bags to each student. Have students label one bag "rocks" and one bag "minerals." Review procedures for appropriate behavior in the "outdoor classroom." Allow students to go outdoors and collect 8–10 rocks and 8–10 minerals. Instruct students to place only rocks in the bag labeled "rocks" and only minerals in the bag labeled "minerals." Encourage students to spread out to ensure adequate coverage of the school grounds. If students do not have access to rocks at your school setting, arrange for samples to be brought into the classroom.

3. Upon returning to the classroom, urge students to carefully observe and record characteristics of the contents of both bags. Students should build a case for why they classified some items rocks and some items minerals.

4. Have students compare and contrast their classifications with at least two others. Allow students to alter their classifications if needed, but retain their original classification schemes.

5. Distribute various minerals to each student, but do not tell students these are minerals. Encourage them to classify the minerals into one of the two sandwich bags. Again, students should build a case for their classification schemes and compare with others.

6. Predictably, there will be disagreement. Use this opportunity to introduce the need to find out how scientists classify rocks and minerals. Focus on this basic question, "What is the difference between the two and how can we/they tell?"

7. Challenge students to research to find the difference between rocks and minerals. Provide trade books, reference materials, field guides, textbooks, and Internet access to aid students in locating information. Encourage students to be prepared to share their sources of information and compare/contrast their findings with others.

8. Ask students to return to their classification schemes. Offer them the chance to reclassify any of the objects and provide reasoning for why they did so. Suggest a new category: "Not Sure," if this is the case. Assure students there will be opportunities to learn and practice rock and mineral identification in upcoming lessons.

Name: _____ Date: _____

Student Inquiry Activity 2 : What's the Difference? (cont.)

Exploration/Data Collection:

1. Record your current understanding of the difference between rocks and minerals.

    _____

    _____

    _____

    _____

    _____

    _____

2. Obtain two sandwich bags and label one "rocks" and one "minerals." With supervision, go outside and collect what you believe to be 8–10 rocks and 8–10 minerals. Record field notes to remind yourself why you placed each sample into each bag.

3. Return indoors and observe the samples carefully. Create a T-Chart with columns labeled "Rocks" and "Minerals." Record observations, descriptors, and reasons why you classified the samples into each bag. Use the space below or your own paper.

Student Inquiry Activity **2**: What's the Difference? (cont.)

4. In what ways does your T-Chart compare with at least two other students' charts? Record your comparisons below.

_____

_____

_____

_____

_____

_____

5. Research to find what scientists believe to be the difference between rocks and minerals. Compare and contrast your findings with those of the scientists' findings. Adjust your classification scheme and T-Chart, if needed (use a different-colored writing instrument).

Summary/What to Look For:
1. To what extent did students accurately define rocks and provide examples?
2. To what extent did students accurately define minerals and provide examples?
3. To what extent did students accurately articulate the differences between rocks and minerals?
4. To what extent did students identify physical characteristics/properties of rocks and minerals?
5. To what extent were students' prior conceptions of the differences between rocks and minerals changed?

Extension and Real-World Applications:
1. If you found a rock/mineral while on a camping trip, how would you determine which it is? Provide a step-by-step description of your procedures.

Discussion Questions/Assessment:
1. Add a paragraph and/or illustration that describes the differences between rocks and minerals to the Rocks and Minerals poster. Include how rocks and minerals on the earth's surface might vary from those on the interior.

2. Cross-reference the paragraph to visually represent the location of rocks and minerals on the Earth model.

3. Return to the K-W-L chart. Examine the columns for additions and editing needs based upon what you have learned during these activities, e.g., in what ways has your thinking changed?

Student Inquiry Activity **3** : Which One Is Which?

Topic: Mineral Identification

Introductory Statement:
Now that you are aware of the difference between rocks and minerals, you will have the opportunity to identify minerals by conducting various tests of their physical properties.

NSES Content Standard D: Structure of the Earth System
The solid earth is layered with a lithosphere; hot, convecting mantle; and dense, metallic core.
Landforms are the result of a combination of constructive and destructive forces. Constructive forces include crustal deformation, volcanic eruption, and deposition of sediment, while destructive forces include weathering and erosion.

Science Skills and Concepts:
- Students will identify minerals according to the physical properties of streak, hardness, luster, cleavage, specific gravity, magnetism, and reaction to acid.
- Students will infer the relationship of crystal formation to minerals.
- Students will construct a model of the silicon-oxygen tetrahedron.
- Students will analyze minerals as they pertain to families.

Materials/Safety Concerns:
Samples of various, common minerals, e.g., fluorite, talc, gypsum, quartz, halite, mica, galena, feldspar, calcite, hornblende, muscovite, pyrite, hematite, orthoclase
Small white porcelain plates, unglazed
Vinegar
Water and graduated cylinders
Pennies
Glass plates (Caution: be sure the edges are ground)
Steel file
Magnets
Safety goggles
8 cm Styrofoam™ balls (4 per student or pair of students)
2 cm Styrofoam™ balls (1 per student or pair of students)
Toothpicks
Markers/crayons/colored pencils/tempera paint

Note: Mineral samples can be obtained from Ward's Geology:

Ward's Scientific
P.O. Box 92912
Rochester, NY 14692-9012
www.wardsci.com
1-800-962-2660

Content Background:
Prior to the study of rocks, it is important for students to be able to apply the processes used to identify some of the minerals found in rocks. Mineralogists commonly use a battery of tests to determine the identity of minerals (streak/color, hardness, luster, cleavage, specific

Student Inquiry Activity 3 : Which One Is Which? (cont.)

gravity, magnetism, and reaction to acid). Many other tests for mineral identification exist, but for the purposes of this activity, students will conduct seven of the more common tests as they identify a mystery mineral.

Although there are over 4,000 known minerals, with new ones being discovered each year, only about 10–12 are abundant. Together, these abundant minerals account for what are known as the **rock-forming minerals**. Interestingly, the rock-forming minerals consist of 8–10 major elements, some of which are: oxygen (O), silicon (Si), iron (Fe), aluminum (Al), calcium (Ca), sodium (Na), potassium (K), and magnesium (Mg). In essence, the vast majority of the earth's crust is made of these major elements in some form.

Minerals can easily be classified into groups known as families. For example, one family of rock-forming minerals is known as the silicates. Silicates have a common crystalline structure, known as the **silicon-oxygen tetrahedron**. Quartz, a silicate, is a very prevalent mineral found in many rocks on the earth's surface. In its pure form, quartz consists entirely of silicon-oxygen tetrahedral. Most other silicates combine with other elements, such as iron, sodium, calcium, potassium, and magnesium.

Other families of minerals include: carbonates, halides, oxides, sulfides, and sulfates. These are considered to be non-silicates and account for only about one-quarter of the earth's continental crust.

Note: This lesson is divided into three parts. Instructors may wish to spread the activities out over several days depending upon time allotments.

Procedures:
Part I—Mineral Identification

1. Ask students to speculate and record how they would proceed to identify a mineral brought to them by a younger friend or sibling. Discuss the students' responses as a large group.

2. Inform the students that they have been hired by the Acme Mineral Company to identify minerals that were mixed together after a large earthquake. To ensure quality control, students will be asked to work in teams. The task is to conduct tests to relabel the minerals.

3. Provide a brief overview of each testing station:

   Streak - Streak should not be confused with the color of the mineral. It is possible for the color of a mineral to vary from the color of the streak it leaves when dragged across a piece of white porcelain plate. The absence of streak should be noted as well; this information should be synthesized with the hardness.

   Hardness - A test for how hard a mineral is; the Mohs' scale consists of ten minerals of varying hardness. The hardness of a mineral can be determined by rubbing an unknown mineral against the known minerals.

Student Inquiry Activity **3** : Which One Is Which? (cont.)

Common objects can be used in place of the mineral on the Mohs' scale, e.g., in case you don't have these minerals while in the field. The common objects are listed in parentheses to the right of the minerals. Students should use common objects for initial tests. Students should determine whether the mineral scratches the object or the object scratches the mineral. The item that scratches is considered to be harder. Safety goggles should be worn for this test.

Mohs' scale

    1 - **Talc** (easily scratched by your fingernail)
    2 - **Gypsum** (can be scratched by your fingernail, 2.5)
    3 - **Calcite** (barely can be scratched by a penny, 3)
    4 - **Fluorite** (easily scratched with a steel file or a piece of glass)
    5 - **Apatite** (can be scratched with a steel file or a piece of glass, 5.5)
    6 - **Orthoclase** (can scratch glass with difficulty)
    7 - **Quartz** (easily scratches both a steel file and glass)
    8 - **Topaz** (scratches quartz)
    9 - **Corundum**
  10 - **Diamond** (scratches everything)

Luster - A test for how light interacts with the surface of the mineral. Observe the mineral for one of the following classifications:

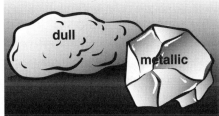

- **Dull** - no reflection of any kind at all
- **Earthy** - looks like dirt or dried mud
- **Fibrous** - appears to have fibers
- **Greasy** - looks like grease; may even feel greasy
- **Metallic** - perhaps shiny with the look of metals
- **Pearly** - looks like a pearl
- **Silky** - looks silky; sometimes hard to differentiate between fibrous; more compact
- **Vitreous** - the most common luster; the look of glass
- **Waxy** - looks like wax

Cleavage - This test is related to the crystalline structure and chemical bonding of the mineral and is determined by close observation of breaks within the sample. Minerals that are considered to have good cleavage tend to split/break uniformly, along planes. For example, micas are made of tetrahedral sheets and break into thin sheets along the lines of the bonds. Galena tends to break into cubes with straight sides. These minerals have good cleavage. Many minerals do not have good cleavage; these are considered to be uneven or irregular and appear to be fractured along uneven planes/lines. In order to preserve the samples, students should not try to break the minerals in any way.

27

Student Inquiry Activity **3** : Which One Is Which? (cont.)

Specific Gravity - This test refers to the weight of an amount of mineral compared to an equal amount of water. The specific gravity of the mineral is sometimes estimated via heft, e.g., lift equal amounts of quartz and galena. For the purposes of this activity, simple water displacement can be used to determine the density of each mineral sample. Most minerals have a density of 2–3 g/cubic cm, but the heavier minerals often have densities as high as 7–20 g/cubic cm. Therefore, density will be more helpful in identifying heavier minerals.

Magnetism - Some minerals contain magnetic properties; this is easily tested by placing the mineral sample near a magnet.

Reaction to Acid - Minerals that react (usually fizzing/bubbling) tend to come from the carbonate family. Students should place a small drop of vinegar on the mineral and observe carefully for any reaction. Safety goggles should be worn for this test.

Management Note: The mineral tests described above will not all take students the same amount of time. If possible, have several stations set up for each test, thereby allowing students to advance and complete more mineral identification.

4. Distribute one mystery mineral (numbered to match an answer key) to each pair of students. Be sure that two pairs of students have the same mineral, for later comparison. Allow five to seven minutes for each test; have students rotate through all seven stations, recording data from each test.

5. Upon completion of the tests, provide field guides and reference materials to assist students in identification of the minerals. Refer students to the website: http://mineral.galleries.com/ for assistance and confirmation of the mineral. Pairs should consult each other for agreement on the identification.

6. Students who work quickly and/or finish early may choose another mineral for identification.

Part II—Quartz Models

1. Review the physical properties of quartz, one of the minerals students identified in Part I. Explain that quartz is a mineral that is considered to be a pure silicate; that is, it contains only the single building block of all silicates, a silicon-oxygen tetrahedron.

2. Some basic chemistry instruction may augment this activity, depending on the developmental ability of the students. At least provide a basic overview of elements, parts of the atom, and ionic bonding (if appropriate).

Student Inquiry Activity 3 : Which One Is Which? (cont.)

3. Lead students as they build a model of the silicon-oxygen tetrahedral. Color the silicon atom one color; color the oxygen atoms another color. Point out that these models represent the two elements and the number of atoms of each (one silicon and four oxygen). Attach the oxygen atoms (equal distance) to the silicon atom via toothpicks. Label each atom with the correct chemical symbol.

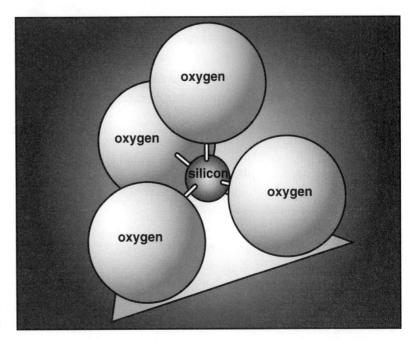

4. Point out that this compound is the basic building block of the rock-forming silicates.

Part III—Mineral Families

1. Instruct students to create a drawing of a large tree with six branches (concept maps and family tree diagrams are suitable replacements).

2. Instruct students to research to find six families of minerals. Provide trade books, reference materials, field guides, textbooks, and Internet access to aid students in locating the information. Encourage students to be prepared to share their sources of information and compare/contrast their findings with others.

3. Each branch should represent one family of minerals and a brief summary of what makes that family unique from the others. Attach numerous leaves containing the name and chemical formula (e.g., galena PbS) of sample minerals from each family to each branch. The trunk of the tree should contain a brief summary of information learned about minerals in general.

4. Challenge students to infer commonalities of minerals within each family.

5. Post students' work to aid in large-group discussion and for comparison of findings.

Name: _____ Date: _____

Student Inquiry Activity 3 : Which One Is Which? (cont.)

Exploration/Data Collection:
Part I—Mineral Identification

1. One day, a younger sibling or friend brings you a mineral and wonders if you would help him/her identify it. Explain what steps you would take to help him/her identify the mineral.

_____

_____

_____

_____

2. Alert! You have been hired by Acme Mineral Company (which happens to be owned by your teacher) to identify minerals that were mixed up after a large earthquake. The president of the company will provide you with mineral samples and instructions for seven tests to help you succeed with this task. Be sure to follow the directions at each test station as you take notes and record your observations at each station. You will use the data collected at each testing station to ultimately determine the identity of the mineral. Good luck!

Station A: Streak

_____

_____

_____

Station B: Hardness

_____

_____

_____

Station C: Luster

_____

_____

_____

Station D: Cleavage

_____

_____

_____

Name: _____   Date: _____

Student Inquiry Activity **3** : Which One Is Which? (cont.)

Station E: Specific Gravity

_____

_____

_____

Station F: Magnetism

_____

_____

_____

Station G: Reaction to Acid

_____

_____

_____

3. Carefully review your notes/observations. Use the reference materials provided by the Acme Mineral Company to make a ruling on the identity of your mystery mineral. Complete the two statements below. Save your results for later discussion.

I/We _____ do hereby certify that mystery min-

eral # _____ is the mineral _____.

Signed _____ Date _____

Witness _____

I/We certify that my/our confidence in this decision is represented by:

   10   9   8   7   6   5   4   3   2   1

Certain   Sure   I think it might be   Not sure   No way!

My/Our reason(s) for this rating is/are: _____

_____

_____

_____

_____

Name: _____ Date: _____

Student Inquiry Activity 3 : Which One Is Which? (cont.)

Part II—The Building Blocks of Minerals/Quartz Models

1. Record the chemical symbols for the elements:

   _____ oxygen   _____ silicon   _____ magnesium   _____ aluminum

   _____ iron   _____ calcium   _____ potassium   _____ sodium

2. Construct a model of the silicon-oxygen tetrahedron, which makes up quartz. Follow the instructions given by your teacher.

3. Write the chemical formula for quartz. _____

4. How does the chemical formula for quartz compare with the silicon-oxygen tetrahedron?

   _____

   _____

   _____

   _____

5. What does this tell you about the chemical make-up of quartz?

   _____

   _____

   _____

   _____

Part III—Mineral Families

1. Visualize a tree and its parts. Create a large representation of a tree. Add the following information:
   - the trunk should contain information you have learned about minerals in general.
   - create at least six branches; label each branch with one of the main families of minerals.
   - add leaves, which represent individual minerals within each family (mineral name and chemical symbol or formula), to each branch.

2. What commonalities do you find within the minerals of each family?

   _____

   _____

   _____

   _____

Name: _____ Date: _____

Student Inquiry Activity **3** : Which One Is Which? (cont.)

3. Compare your tree with others. How is it like the other trees? How is it different?

_____

_____

_____

_____

4. List several ideas about minerals that you saw on others' work but were not found on yours.

_____

_____

_____

_____

Summary/What to Look For:
1. To what extent did students accurately identify minerals according to the physical properties of streak, hardness, luster, cleavage, specific gravity, magnetism, and reaction to acid?
2. To what extent did students accurately infer the relationship of crystal formation to minerals?
3. To what extent did students accurately construct a model of the silicon-oxygen tetrahedron?
4. To what extent were students able to analyze minerals as they pertain to families?

Extension and Real-World Applications:
1. Research to find the family of the mineral(s) you identified for Acme Mineral Company.

Discussion Questions/Assessment:
1. Draw a picture of the silicon-oxygen tetrahedron on your poster. Label each part and provide a brief summary of the importance of the silicon-oxygen tetrahedron in rock-forming minerals.

2. Trace the continents onto your Earth model. Color/paint the water blue and the land green and/or brown. Record the eight major elements that make up most of the rock-forming minerals on a *toothpick flag, and attach the toothpick flag to North America.

3. Return to the K-W-L chart. Examine the columns for additions and editing needs based upon what you have learned during these activities, e.g., in what ways has your thinking changed?

* Toothpick flags/signs can easily be constructed by gluing two small squares of paper back-to-back with a toothpick in between. Computer users can word-process the information and reduce the font to fit the small flag. The toothpick can then be stuck into the Earth model.

Student Inquiry Activity 4 : Animal, Vegetable, or Mineral

Topic: Uses of Minerals

Introductory Statement:

Without minerals, we would not enjoy many goods and services afforded to us in every-day life. These activities are designed to provide a closer look at the importance of minerals in our society.

NSES Content Standard D: Structure of the Earth System

The solid earth is layered with a lithosphere; hot, convecting mantle; and dense, metallic core.

Landforms are the result of a combination of constructive and destructive forces. Constructive forces include crustal deformation, volcanic eruption, and deposition of sediment, while destructive forces include weathering and erosion.

NSES Content Standard E: Understanding About Science and Technology

Scientific inquiry and technological design have similarities and differences. Scientists propose explanations for questions about the natural world, and engineers propose solutions relating to human problems, needs, and aspirations. Technological solutions are temporary; technologies exist within nature, so they cannot contravene physical or biological principles; technological solutions have side effects; and technologies carry risks and provide benefits.

Science Skills and Concepts:
• Students will differentiate between organic and inorganic materials.
• Students will identify applications of minerals in the everyday world.
• Students will classify objects according to animal, vegetable, or mineral.

Materials/Safety Concerns:
Chart paper
Miscellaneous items from the classroom, e.g., stapler, paper, paper clip, rubber band, bounce ball, textbook, chalk, etc.

Content Background:

Minerals serve as raw materials for most of the manufactured goods and services we enjoy as a society. Think about a single sector of our society, such as transportation. Consider the role of minerals in the manufacturing and production of automobiles, trucks, airplanes, trains and rail systems, ships, roads, bridges, and computers within travel agencies. Students may not necessarily connect manufactured goods with minerals. This lesson is designed to increase awareness of the importance of minerals in our everyday lives. It also provides an excellent opportunity to reinforce the importance of science and technology in our society.

A simple way to approach the prevalence of minerals in our society is to classify matter as either animal, vegetable, or mineral. It is difficult to think of matter on our earth that does not fit into one of these three categories.

Student Inquiry Activity ▪️4▪️ : Animal, Vegetable, or Mineral (cont.)

Recall the definition/criteria for description of minerals:
- minerals occur naturally
- minerals are inorganic
- minerals are solids
- minerals have a single chemical composition/structure.

Since minerals are inorganic, this rules out plants and/or animals. What is left must contain minerals of some sort. Although they occur naturally, minerals are often combined to produce goods and services; steel is an excellent example. Students may mistakenly consider steel as a mineral. A review of the rules for minerals (they must occur naturally) will result in the realization that although steel is important, it is not a mineral. However, students should infer that a critical ingredient of steel is the element iron, which appears in the mineral hematite.

Procedures:

1. Review the criteria for classification of substances as minerals (see above). Explain that this activity is designed to try to discover the applications of minerals in our everyday lives.

2. Complete the brief review activity and urge students to substantiate their beliefs. Discuss the results as a large group.

3. Ask students to create a list of minerals that they used since they awoke that morning. Encourage students to share their lists (either in small groups or as a class) and explain why they included the items. Allow students to edit their lists as a result of the follow-up discussion.

4. As a homework assignment, ask students to identify 10–12 items from their homes that contain at least one mineral; three to four of the items must be located outdoors. In addition, students should list the minerals contained in each item and their rationale for the classification. Repeat the process for non-mineral items.

5. The next day, compile the results of the mineral scavenger hunt. Create a large wall chart and/or mural for data gathering and comparison. Discuss any items that are in question, and seek consensus for their status. Allow for open-ended inquiries that may require further research.

Name: _____ Date: _____

Student Inquiry Activity ◼4 : Animal, Vegetable, or Mineral (cont.)

Exploration/Data Collection:

1. Write four characteristics all minerals must have.

   _____

   _____

   _____

   _____

2. Write "Y" for yes if the substance is a mineral. Write "N" for no if the substance is not a mineral. Directly under each item, explain why you chose either "Y" or "N."

   ____ steel    ____ glass

   ____ limestone    ____ coal

   ____ skin    ____ gold

   ____ tire   ____ diamond

3. Think back to when you first awoke this morning, and retrace your steps. On your own paper, create a list of everything you came into contact with that contained a mineral or minerals. Be prepared to compare and share your list with others.

36

Name: _____ Date: _____

Student Inquiry Activity 4 : Animal, Vegetable, or Mineral (cont.)

4. Homework Assignment:

    Part I - Go home and identify 10–12 items (not on your original list from Question #3) that contain minerals. Three to four of the items must be found outside your house. Beside each item, write what minerals you believe are contained and how you know this is the case.

    Part II - Next, identify 10–12 items in your home that you believe are not minerals or do not contain minerals. Three to four must be found outside your house. Beside each item, write why you believe this is the case.

Summary/What to Look For:
1. To what extent were students able to accurately differentiate between organic and inorganic materials?
2. To what extent were students able to accurately identify applications of minerals in the everyday world?
3. To what extent were students able to classify objects/items according to animal, vegetable, or mineral?

Extension and Real-World Applications:
1. Urge students to plan a dream vacation. Identify goods and services related to the vacation that contain minerals.

Discussion Questions/Assessment:
1. Based upon what you know about minerals, write "true" or "false" and explain your reasoning.

    "If you can't grow it, it must be a mineral." _____

    _____

    _____

    _____

    _____

2. Earth model - Construct recognizable objects that contain minerals and add them to your Earth model. Cross-reference a description of what you built on the poster, e.g., further explain what you added to the model and why.

3. Return to the K-W-L chart. Examine the columns for additions and editing needs based upon what you have learned during these activities, e.g., in what ways has your thinking changed?

Student Inquiry Activity 5 : Hot Rocks!

Topic: Igneous Rocks

Introductory Statement:
The earth is composed of three major classifications of rocks. In these activities, you will discover igneous rocks, how they are formed, and where they are located in our world today.

> **NSES Content Standard D: Structure of the Earth System**
> Some changes in the solid earth can be described as the rock cycle. Old rocks at the earth's surface weather, forming sediments that are buried, then compacted, heated, and often recrystallized into new rock. Eventually, those new rocks may be brought to the surface by the forces that drive plate motion, and the rock cycle continues.
> Landforms are the result of a combination of constructive and destructive forces. Constructive forces include crustal deformation, volcanic eruption, and deposition of sediment, while destructive forces include weathering and erosion.

Science Skills and Concepts:
- Students will describe the physical properties of igneous rocks.
- Students will infer the relationship between volcanism and igneous rock formation.
- Students will identify igneous rocks within three families.
- Students will associate igneous rock formation with geographical location.
- Students will infer the relationship between silica content and the viscosity of magma.

Materials/Safety Concerns:

9 x 13-inch cake pans (or suitable substitute)
Peanut butter
Molasses
Murphy's™ Oil Soap
Igneous rock samples
Medicine dropper
Small condiment cups
Vegetable oil
Honey
5 x 7-inch sheets of cardboard
Stop watches

Content Background:
Ideally, the study of rocks is best suited within the context of the rock cycle. The lessons in this book are designed to examine each major classification (igneous, sedimentary, and metamorphic) individually, followed by an activity regarding the rock cycle and associated earth movements.

Earlier, students learned that rocks are aggregates of minerals. This lesson is designed to focus on a specific type of rock, igneous rocks. **Igneous rocks** are one of the three major classifications of rocks (see also sedimentary and metamorphic). The formation of igneous rocks is typically associated with plate boundaries: volcanism and sea-floor spreading. In reality, the rocks exist in molten form within the earth (upper mantle/asthenosphere). Molten rock is known as **magma** and is converted into **lava** as it is extruded onto the earth's surface to cool.

Physical properties of igneous rocks are largely determined by the rate at which the rocks cool and the manner in which they are extruded. Slowly cooling lava results in larger,

Student Inquiry Activity 5 : Hot Rocks! (cont.)

more definitive crystals, whereas rapidly cooling crystals are often so small they can't be seen with the naked eye. Geologists use crystal size and arrangement as clues to the conditions under which igneous rocks were formed.

The mineral composition of igneous rocks is dictated by the parent magma from which it cools. Like minerals, rocks can also be classified into families. Igneous rocks are commonly divided into three families:

- **felics** - high in silica content (+65%); light-colored by virtue of their main minerals, which include orthoclastic feldspar, mica, and quartz; rock examples include rhyolite and granites.

Rhyolite   Granite

- **mafics** - high in iron and magnesium; lower in silica content (45–55%); usually darker in color; main minerals include plagioclastic feldspar, olivine, and pyroxene; rock examples include basalts and gabbros.

Basalt   Gabbro

- **intermediates** - contain 55–65% silica; medium color; main minerals include hornblende, biotite mica, and pyroxene; example rocks include andesite and diorite.

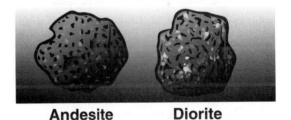

Andesite   Diorite

Viscosity is an important consideration of the nature of molten rock. **Viscosity** is internal resistance to flow within a liquid. Magmas with high viscosity tend to contain higher amounts of silica and commonly form lighter-colored igneous rocks. The highly viscous magma often builds up under intense pressure and is associated with spectacular volcanic eruptions. Low viscosity basalts, which contain less silica, are commonly associated with sea-floor spreading as thin magma oozes through the earth's surface.

Procedures:

1. Refer to the K-W-L chart(s) and briefly review the information learned about the difference between rocks and minerals. Indicate that the next three lessons will focus on the three major classifications of rocks: igneous, sedimentary, and metamorphic. This lesson contains activities regarding igneous rocks.

Student Inquiry Activity 5 : Hot Rocks! (cont.)

2. Ask students to record their current understanding of what is meant by igneous rocks. Provide the Latin origin of the word *igneous* (*ignis,* "fire"). Allow students to edit their responses based upon this clue.

3. Ask students to predict where they would go (currently in the world) to collect igneous rocks. Have students substantiate their explanations. Volcanoes may be a common response; observe if any students refer to sea-floor spreading. This may provide insight into their current understanding of plate tectonics, a related concept that will be investigated in an upcoming lesson.

4. Briefly review the three main states of matter. Ask students under which they would classify rocks and have them defend their views. Observe to see if any students classify rocks as liquids; if so, in what context? Begin to focus the lesson on the liquid form of igneous rocks.

5. Ask students to differentiate between magma and lava. Turn their attention to magma and its characteristics. Introduce the term *viscosity* and how it is related to magma. Indicate that one key factor that influences the viscosity of magma is the amount of silica (review from minerals, if needed).

6. Distribute 5 x 7-inch sheets of cardboard, small cups of honey, Murphy's™ oil soap, and vegetable oil. Entertain students' ideas about how we test the flow of these substances. At this point, it is not necessary to inform students of what the substances are; simply assign random numbers, e.g., #1, #2, #3, etc.

7. Conduct rate of flow tests by arranging the cardboard at a 45 degree angle (within a cake pan). Create a starting point and an ending point in order to time the flow of the substance. Be sure to discuss variables and the concept of a fair test. Allow students to create a hypothesis before testing. Encourage students to be prepared to share their findings with the class.

8. Using aggregated data, determine an order of viscosity for the three substances. Draw the analogy to magma with varying amounts of silica. Provide samples of rocks from each of the three igneous families: rhyolite, andesite, and basalt work well. Ask students to infer the relationship between color and the amount of silica.

9. Challenge students to predict what would happen if the process were to be repeated, but at higher temperatures, e.g., warm the substances in a microwave. Perhaps test other substances in this manner as well, e.g., peanut butter. Students should infer that the temperature of magma is another key factor related to its viscosity.

10. Provide samples of additional igneous rocks for identification using field guides and reference materials. Urge students to consider color as they classify.

Name: _____ Date: _____

Student Inquiry Activity **5** : Hot Rocks! (cont.)

Exploration/Data Collection:

1. Briefly describe the difference between rocks and minerals.

   _____

   _____

   _____

   _____

2. Pretend a large cash award was available for those who could retrieve an igneous rock. Where would you go to get an igneous rock, and how would you make sure it was an igneous rock?

   _____

   _____

   _____

3. What do you think is the difference between lava and magma?

   _____

   _____

   _____

4. My definition of viscosity is: _____

   _____

   _____

The Liquid Race:

1. In a cake pan, prop the cardboard sheet you have been given at a 45 degree angle. Draw a start (near the top) and stop line (near the bottom). The objective of the race is to determine the speed at which each substance flows down the race board and determine an order of viscosity.

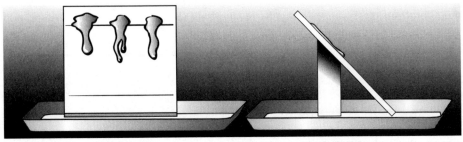

Front view   **Side view**

Name: _____ Date: _____

Student Inquiry Activity 5 : Hot Rocks! (cont.)

2. My hypothesis for the rate of flow is:

_____

_____

_____

3. Variables that will need to be controlled include:

_____

_____

_____

4. The methods I will follow during the test include:

_____

_____

_____

_____

_____

_____

_____

5. My observations and data (times) include:

_____

_____

_____

_____

6. Look back at your hypothesis; what can you conclude?

_____

_____

_____

_____

_____

Name: _____ Date: _____

Student Inquiry Activity 5 : Hot Rocks! (cont.)

7. I predict the names of these substances are:

   _____

   _____

8. What are some possible ways to increase/decrease the viscosity of the substances?

   _____

   _____

   _____

   _____

9. What are other possibilities for tests regarding the viscosity of a liquid? If materials are available, contact your teacher for further testing.

Summary/What to Look For:
1. To what extent did students accurately describe the physical properties of igneous rocks?
2. To what extent did students accurately infer the relationship between volcanism and igneous rock formation?
3. To what extent did students accurately identify igneous rocks within three families?
4. To what extent did students accurately associate igneous rock formation with geographical location?
5. To what extent did students accurately infer the relationship between silica content and the viscosity of magma?

Discussion Questions/Assessment:
1. Illustrate where you would likely find igneous rocks on your Earth model. Perhaps build and attach a small volcano. Attach toothpick flags with information that explains igneous rock formation and gives examples. Cross-reference this information to your poster.

2. On your poster, create a cross-sectional diagram of the formation and release of igneous rocks as they enter the earth's surface. Provide a written explanation that further explains your drawing. Be creative in your description and drawings.

3. Return to the K-W-L chart. Examine the columns for additions and editing needs based upon what you have learned during these activities, e.g., in what ways has your thinking changed?

Student Inquiry Activity **6**: Heat + Pressure = Metamorphic Rocks

Topic: Metamorphic Rocks

Introductory Statement:

The earth is composed of three major classifications of rocks. In these activities, you will discover metamorphic rocks, how they are formed, and how they differ from igneous rocks.

> **NSES Content Standard D: Structure of the Earth System**
>
> Some changes in the solid earth can be described as the rock cycle. Old rocks at the earth's surface weather, forming sediments that are buried, then compacted, heated, and often recrystallized into new rock. Eventually, those new rocks may be brought to the surface by the forces that drive plate motions, and the rock cycle continues.
>
> Landforms are the result of a combination of constructive and destructive forces. Constructive forces include crustal deformation, volcanic eruption, and deposition of sediment, while destructive forces include weathering and erosion.

Science Skills and Concepts:
- Students will describe the physical properties of metamorphic rocks.
- Students will infer the catalysts for metamorphic rock formation.
- Students will identify metamorphic rocks within two families.
- Students will associate metamorphic rock formation with geographical location.
- Students will infer the relationship between metamorphic and igneous rock formation.

Materials/Safety Concerns:

Rolling pin or 1-inch dowel rods	Honey
Graham crackers	Butterscotch chips
Chocolate bars	Raisins
Mini-marshmallows	Coconut
Resealable bags	Samples of metamorphic rocks
Paper towels	Plastic gloves

Content Background:

Metamorphism means "change," within the context of rocks. Heat, pressure, and chemically active fluids that contain chemicals can convert mineral composition in rocks, thereby forming new, different rocks. Metamorphism can occur beneath the surface of the earth, where the magma from the asthenosphere comes into contact with the bottom of the crust of the earth. Here, heat is the greatest metamorphic agent. Tremendous amounts of heat and pressure can also be found along plate lines that are converging. Ultimately, metamorphism causes chemical changes in the composition of the rocks. Metamorphism can occur to varying degrees depending upon the levels/amounts of heat, pressure, and chemically active fluids.

Two general classifications (families) of metamorphic rocks include **foliated** (rocks with layered bands) and **non-foliated** (rocks without layered bands). Foliated rocks are not to be confused with basic sedimentary rocks, although some parallel principles apply. Common

44

Student Inquiry Activity 6: Heat + Pressure = Metamorphic Rocks (cont.)

examples of foliated metamorphic rocks include slate, schist, and gneiss. Common examples of non-foliated metamorphic rocks include marble and quartzite.

Top: foliated slate
Bottom: non-foliated marble

Procedures:

1. Refer to the K-W-L chart(s) and briefly review the information learned about the difference between rocks and minerals. Indicate that this is the second of three lessons that focus on one of the three major classifications of rocks: igneous, metamorphic, and sedimentary. This lesson contains activities regarding metamorphic rocks.

2. Ask students to record their current understanding of what is meant by metamorphic rocks. Introduce the word *metamorphosis* and discuss its meaning. Allow students to edit their responses based upon this clue.

3. Ask students to predict where they would go (currently in the world) to collect metamorphic rocks. Have students substantiate their explanations.

4. Guide students as they build metamorphic s'mores. Layer graham crackers, mini-marshmallows, butterscotch chips, chocolate bars, coconut, honey (small amount), and raisins. Ask students to infer what each ingredient represents:
    *   graham crackers and chocolate bars: layers of rock
    *   mini-marshmallows, butterscotch chips, and raisins: smaller chunks of rock
    *   coconut: organic debris
    *   honey: chemically active liquid

5. Record observations of the model. Place the layered s'more in a resealable bag and wrap it in a paper towel. Use a rolling pin or dowel rod to compress the ingredients. Compare and contrast the metamorphic s'more before and after the pressure was applied.

6. Ask students to predict what would happen if heat were applied to the compressed metamorphic s'more, e.g., toaster oven or microwave oven. Point out that in addition to pressure, a tremendous amount of heat is a key ingredient in the formation of metamorphic rocks. Ask students to infer the source of heat needed to melt rocks.

7. A more difficult inference is the role of chemically active liquids (honey). Simply explain that in combination, these factors result in new rocks with different chemical composition.

8. Distribute cups of crumbled metamorphic s'mores and enjoy a snack while observing samples of metamorphic rocks. Provide field guides and reference materials for identification of samples. Urge students to classify foliated and non-foliated metamorphic rocks.

45

Name: _____ Date: _____

Student Inquiry Activity **6** : Heat + Pressure = Metamorphic Rocks (cont.)

Exploration/Data Collection:

1. Briefly describe the difference between rocks and minerals.

   _____

   _____

   _____

2. Pretend a large cash award was available for those who could retrieve a metamorphic rock. Where would you go to get a metamorphic rock, and how would you make sure it was a metamorphic rock?

   _____

   _____

   _____

   _____

3. *Metamorphic* comes from the word *metamorphosis.* Write a definition, in your own words.

   _____

   _____

Metamorphic S'mores:

1. Create a metamorphic s'more using layers of graham cracker, mini-marshmallow, raisins, chocolate bars, honey, butterscotch chips, and coconut. Draw a diagram of your s'more.

2. Predict what each ingredient might represent within metamorphic rock.

   graham crackers _____

   mini-marshmallows _____

   raisins _____

   chocolate bars _____

   honey _____

   butterscotch chips _____

   coconut _____

Name: _____ Date: _____

Student Inquiry Activity 6: Heat + Pressure = Metamorphic Rocks (cont.)

3. Place the metamorphic s'more into a resealable bag. Use a rolling pin or dowel rod to carefully and evenly apply pressure to the metamorphic s'more. Record your observations in drawing form; compare and contrast the metamorphic s'more before and after pressure was applied.

4. Predict what would happen to the compressed metamorphic s'more if it were heated (cooked). Record your prediction in drawing form.

Summary/What to Look For:
1. To what extent were students able to accurately describe the physical properties of metamorphic rock?
2. To what extent were students able to accurately infer the catalysts for metamorphic rock formation?
3. To what extent were students able to accurately identify metamorphic rocks within two families?
4. To what extent were students able to accurately associate metamorphic rock formation with geographical location?
5. To what extent were students able to accurately infer the relationship between metamorphic and igneous rock formation?

Extension and Real-World Applications:
1. Challenge students to identify other phenomena in which metamorphosis takes place. What commonalities are there with metamorphic rocks? What differences exist?

Discussion Questions/Assessment:
1. Illustrate where you would likely find metamorphic rocks on your Earth model. Perhaps build and attach a series of mountains, particularly in North America. Attach toothpick flags with information that explains metamorphic rock formation and give examples. Cross-reference this information to your poster.
2. On your poster, create a cross-sectional diagram of a metamorphic rock formation, e.g., a road-cut. Provide a caption that explains how these rocks are formed. Be creative in your drawings and explanations.
3. Return to the K-W-L chart. Examine the columns for additions and editing needs based upon what you have learned during these activities, e.g., in what ways has your thinking changed?

Student Inquiry Activity **7** : Settle Down!

Topic: Sedimentary Rocks

Introductory Statement:

The earth is composed of three major classifications of rocks. In these activities you will discover sedimentary rocks, how they are formed, and where they are located in our world today.

NSES Content Standard D: Structure of the Earth System

Some changes in the solid earth can be described as the rock cycle. Old rocks at the earth's surface weather, forming sediments that are buried, then compacted, heated, and often recrystallized into new rock. Eventually, those new rocks may be brought to the surface by the forces that drive plate motions, and the rock cycle continues.

Landforms are the result of a combination of constructive and destructive forces. Constructive forces include crustal deformation, volcanic eruption, and deposition of sediment, while destructive forces include weathering and erosion.

Science Skills and Concepts:
- Students will describe the physical properties of sedimentary rocks (three families).
- Students will infer the relationship between weathering and erosion and sedimentary rock formation.
- Students will identify sedimentary rocks and classify them into three families.
- Students will associate sedimentary rock formation with geographical location.
- Students will infer the main ingredients of sedimentary rocks.

Materials/Safety Concerns:

Ample amounts of sand, gravel, pea gravel, clay soil, topsoil
Clear peanut butter jars (or a suitable replacement; must have a tightly fitting lid)
Water
Samples of sedimentary rocks

Content Background:

Sedimentary rocks are formed by the weathering and erosion of existing rocks. This process results from physical and chemical forces in nature, which are responsible for three main classifications of sedimentary rocks:

- **Chemical sedimentary rocks:** formed via dissolved minerals that either settle out (precipitate), e.g., limestone, or evaporate from liquids, e.g., halite and gypsum

Limestone   **Halite**   **Gypsum**

Student Inquiry Activity **7**: Settle Down! (cont.)

- **Clastic sedimentary rocks:** classified by the size of particles that have been transported via wind, moving water, and erosion; conglomerates (round, cemented, gravel-sized particles), breccias (angular fragments imply that particles didn't travel far), sandstones (contain sands), and shales (muds)

| Conglomerate | Breccia | Sandstone |

- **Organic sedimentary rocks:** contain the remains of materials that were once alive; high in carbon; examples include coal and organic limestone

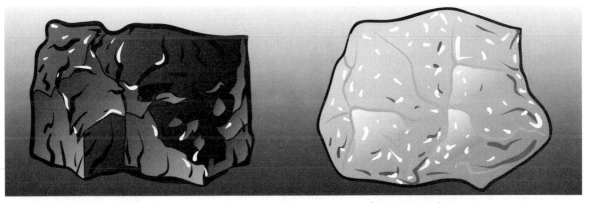

| Coal | Organic Limestone |

In all cases, two common processes occur: compaction and cementation. **Compaction** is caused by the weight of the overlying rocks and provides the impetus for literally squeezing the sediments together. **Cementation** is a chemical process through which water carries and deposits dissolved minerals in the small spaces between the sediment particles. In a sense, the particles are cemented together.

Sedimentary rocks are known for their layered characteristics and often provide clues to the past in the form of fossils. Sedimentary rocks can commonly be observed at road-cuts along various highways and along many roads leading down into river valleys. Although sedimentary rocks make up only a slight fraction (one-twentieth) of the upper 16 meters of the earth's crust, they account for roughly three-fourths of the rock outcroppings in the earth's surface (Tarbuck & Lutgens, 1997).

Student Inquiry Activity **7** : Settle Down! (cont.)

Procedures:

1. Refer to the K-W-L chart(s) and briefly review the information learned about the difference between rocks and minerals. Indicate that this is the third of three lessons that focus on the three major classifications of rocks: igneous, metamorphic, and sedimentary. This lesson contains activities regarding sedimentary rocks.

2. Ask students to record their current understanding of what is meant by sedimentary rocks. Provide the Latin origin of the word, *sedimentary* (*sedimentum,* "settle"). Allow students to edit their responses based upon this clue.

3. Ask students to predict where they would go (currently in the world) to collect sedimentary rocks. Have students substantiate their explanations.

4. Distribute peanut butter jars and rock and soil materials (sand, gravel, pea gravel, topsoil, clay soil).

5. Instruct students to place equal amounts (in volume) of each substance in the jar. No particular order is required. The rock and soil materials should account for roughly 60% of the volume of the jar. Fill the remaining 40% with water; fasten the lid tightly and shake vigorously for several minutes.

6. Encourage students to record observations of the materials and create drawings of what the jars look like with all of the rock and soil materials mixed together (side view). Set the jars aside where they will not be disturbed.

7. Recheck the jars every two to three hours, recording observations and notes regarding changes over time. Do this for several days, until it is clear there are no more changes.

8. Encourage students to share their findings with others. Compare and contrast the drawings and observations from initial construction to the last observation. Introduce the word *stratification;* ask students to infer what this means. As clues, provide samples of sedimentary rock with distinctive lithification.

9. Lead a class discussion of sedimentary rocks and how they are formed; relate the settling jars to the long-term formation of sedimentary rocks. Ask students to infer what caused the layers to form as they did. Urge them to infer what this observation might have to do with the formation of sedimentary rocks. Discuss where sedimentary rocks are likely to be found.

10. Provide field guides and reference materials for the identification of sedimentary rock samples. Urge students to classify clastic, chemical, and organic sedimentary rocks.

Name: _____ Date: _____

Student Inquiry Activity **7** : Settle Down! (cont.)

Exploration/Data Collection:

1. Briefly describe the difference between rocks and minerals.

   _____

   _____

   _____

   _____

2. Pretend a large cash award was available for those who could retrieve a sedimentary rock. Where would you go to get a sedimentary rock, and how would you make sure it was a sedimentary rock?

   _____

   _____

   _____

   _____

   _____

3. Sedimentary comes from the Latin word *sedimentum,* which means "to settle." Write a definition in your own words.

   _____

   _____

   _____

Settle Down!

1. Using materials provided by your teacher, place equal amounts (in volume) of sand, gravel, pea gravel, clay soil, and topsoil in an empty jar. The rocks and soils should take up roughly 60% of the total volume of the jar. Fill the remaining 40% of the jar with water. Fasten the lid **tightly** and shake vigorously for several minutes. Record your observations of the contents of the jar; use sketches as well.

   _____

   _____

   _____

   _____

   _____

   _____

Sketches

Name: _____ Date: _____

Student Inquiry Activity 7 : Settle Down! (cont.)

2. Set the jars aside where they will not be disturbed.

3. Recheck the jars every two to three hours, recording observations and notes regarding changes over time. Do this for several days, until it is clear there are no more changes. Use your own paper for further drawings if needed.

	Sketches
_____	

4. Compare and contrast your findings with others.

Name: _____ Date: _____

Student Inquiry Activity **7** : Settle Down! (cont.)

Summary/What to Look For:

1. To what extent were students able to accurately describe the physical properties (three families) of sedimentary rocks?
2. To what extent were students able to accurately infer the relationship between weathering and erosion and sedimentary rock formation?
3. To what extent were students able to accurately identify sedimentary rocks and classify them into the three families?
4. To what extent were students able to accurately associate sedimentary rock formation with geographical location?
5. To what extent were students able to accurately infer the main ingredients of sedimentary rocks?

Extension and Real-World Applications:

1. Depending upon your geographical location, locate a road-cut that clearly shows sedimentary rock layers. Arrange for a field trip to the location; perhaps arrange for a geologist to provide an interpretation of the rock formation.

Discussion Questions/Assessment:

1. Add a sedimentary rock formation to your Earth model, perhaps near a major river. Insert toothpick flags to further explain your intended information. Cross-reference the information to the poster.

2. Add a cross-sectional diagram of clastic, chemical, and organic sedimentary rock formations. Explain the conditions under which each are formed. Be creative in your drawings and descriptions.

3. Return to the K-W-L chart. Examine the columns for additions and editing needs based upon what you have learned during these activities, e.g., in what ways has your thinking changed?

Student Inquiry Activity 8 : Around and Around

Topic: The Rock Cycle

Introductory Statement:

During the past three lessons, you have learned about the characteristics of three major classifications of rocks and how they are formed. In these activities, you will discover how the three major types of rocks are related to each other.

NSES Content Standard D: Structure of the Earth System

Some changes in the solid earth can be described as the rock cycle. Old rocks at the earth's surface weather, forming sediments that are buried, then compacted, heated, and often recrystallized into new rock. Eventually, those new rocks may be brought to the surface by the forces that drive plate motions, and the rock cycle continues.

Landforms are the result of a combination of constructive and destructive forces. Constructive forces include crustal deformation, volcanic eruption, and deposition of sediment, while destructive forces include weathering and erosion.

Lithospheric plates on the scales of continents and oceans constantly move at rates of centimeters per year in response to movements in the mantle. Major geological events, such as earthquakes, volcanic eruptions, and mountain building, result from these plate motions.

Science Skills and Concepts:
• Students will infer the processes necessary for the rock cycle to occur.
• Students will analyze the role of plate tectonics in the rock cycle.
• Students will describe how rocks can be converted into other forms of rocks.

Materials/Safety Concerns:
Field guides and reference materials regarding rocks and the rock cycle
Various colors of modeling clay
Composition paper
Internet access

Content Background:

Rocks are formed in a cycle. **Igneous rocks** are formed as magma is extruded and cooled in hotspots, volcanoes, and in sea-floor spreading. When exposed rocks become subjected to elements, such as wind, rain, sun, freezing, thawing, glaciers, etc., they break into smaller parts and are often transported where they are deposited in layers. When the layers are subjected to tremendous pressure, **sedimentary rocks** are formed. Rocks may become **metamorphic** if the pressure is great enough and intense heat is present over time to produce a chemical change in the rocks. The rocks may even melt and become part of the magma once again. It is important to realize that rocks do not always go through all three phases of the rock cycle. For example, igneous rocks may become metamorphosed beneath the surface of the earth without ever being broken down into sediment.

Student Inquiry Activity 8 : Around and Around (cont.)

The rock cycle takes place both on continental and oceanic crust and includes the inner workings of the earth. Central to the rock cycle is the concept of **plate tectonics**, the catalyst for volcanoes, hotspots, and sea-floor spreading. These movements are critical steps in introducing magma to the earth's surface. Equally important are convergent plate boundaries, whereby more dense oceanic crust is thrust under lighter, less dense continental crust. It is at these convergent plate boundaries that oceanic crust is literally recycled by virtue of tremendous heat and pressure, which ultimately result in melting as the crust reenters the magma of the asthenosphere.

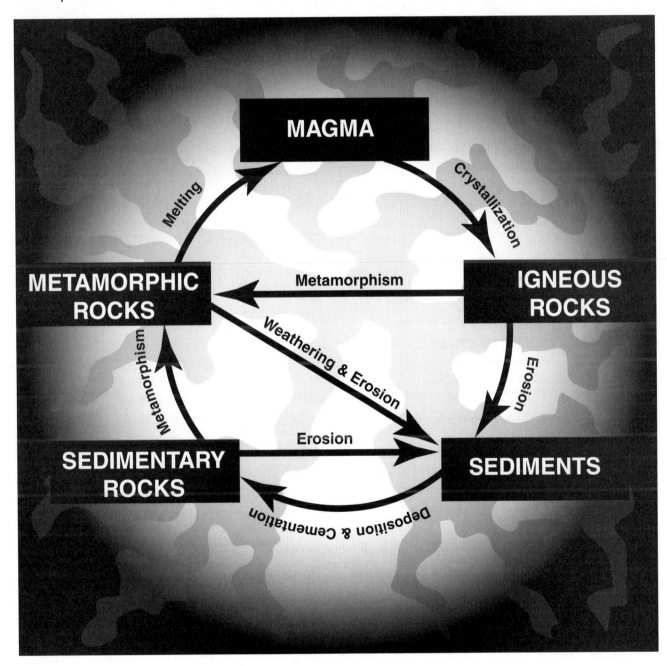

Student Inquiry Activity 8 : Around and Around (cont.)

Procedures:
Part I

1. Ask students to explain the following question:

    "Why don't volcanoes eventually empty the inside of the earth, e.g, if they keep erupting, one would assume that eventually the internal part of the earth would become empty?"

2. Prepare a globe with major plates identified. Use the globe to describe the basic concept of *plate tectonics. Include the concept of convection currents. Focus on convergent and divergent plate boundaries, although it is important to allude to lateral plate movements, e.g., earthquakes.

    *For an excellent curriculum resource regarding plate tectonics, see *Plate Tectonics, The Way the Earth Works* (for complete reference information, see Curriculum Resources in the back of the book).

3. Provide modeling clay for students to create three-dimensional models of convergent and divergent plate boundaries.

4. As a lead-in to Part II, ask students to discuss how plate boundaries might relate to rock formation.

Part II

1. Lead a large-group discussion focusing on the nature of cycles. Ask students to provide examples of cycles in nature.

2. Ask students to recall the individual rock-forming processes of each of the three major rock classifications (igneous, metamorphic, sedimentary).

3. Challenge students to piece the individual rock-forming processes into a larger overall rock cycle. Provide geology reference materials used for the previous investigations of the three major rock classifications. Encourage students to research and find evidence to support their views.

4. Assign students to compose a story, written from the perspective of a rock as it passes through all three forms: igneous, metamorphic, and sedimentary. (Point out that this is usually the case but that some rocks only go through two stages.) Urge students to be descriptive and creative, e.g., describe what is happening to you, what conditions are present as this is happening, etc. Illustrations are welcomed, especially if they help explain the narrative.

5. Allow students to select a starting spot on the rock cycle; this will most likely vary widely.

6. Instruct students to be prepared to share their stories and illustrations with the others; classmates may ask questions as desired.

Name: _____ Date: _____

Student Inquiry Activity 8 : Around and Around (cont.)

Exploration/Data Collection:

1. Please respond to the following question: "Why don't volcanoes eventually empty the inside of the earth? If they keep erupting, one would assume that eventually the internal part of the earth would become empty."

   _____

   _____

   _____

   _____

   _____

2. Using modeling clay, construct a representation of:
   - a convergent plate boundary
   - a divergent plate boundary

3. In your own words, record what scientists believe causes the plates on the earth to move. Observe the model carefully, as you will be adding this concept to your Earth model.

   _____

   _____

   _____

   _____

   _____

   _____

I Am a Rock ...

1. Select your favorite rock and write a story that tells of your experiences as you travel through the rock cycle (one complete cycle). Feel free to use reference materials provided by your instructor to guide you along the way. Be descriptive of the conditions you face and the processes you undergo. Illustrations would greatly assist the reader to understand your life. Use your own paper for this story.

Name: _____ Date: _____

Student Inquiry Activity 8: Around and Around (cont.)

Summary/What to Look For:
1. To what extent did students accurately infer the processes necessary for the rock cycle to occur?
2. To what extent did students accurately analyze the role of plate tectonics in the rock cycle?
3. To what extent did students accurately describe how rocks can be converted into other forms of rock?

Extension and Real-World Applications:
1. Challenge students to identify and explain other cycles found in nature. What commonalities exist between these and the rock cycle? In what ways are they different?
2. Convert creative stories into a script for a play; assign roles and create costumes that relate to the rock cycle.

Discussion Questions/Assessment:
1. Outline at least seven major plates on your Earth model. Add convergent and divergent plate boundaries (both side view and top view). Insert toothpick flags to help explain your intended information. Use the clay model created in a previous activity for clues.
2. Add a diagram of the rock cycle to your poster. Label each major type of rock and include processes that are present within each phase of the rock cycle.
3. Add a diagram of convergent and divergent plate boundaries to your poster. Include captions that explain the processes represented. Cross-reference the information to the Earth model.
4. Return to the K-W-L chart. Examine the columns for additions and editing needs based upon what you have learned during these activities, e.g., in what ways has your thinking changed?

The Tectonic Plates

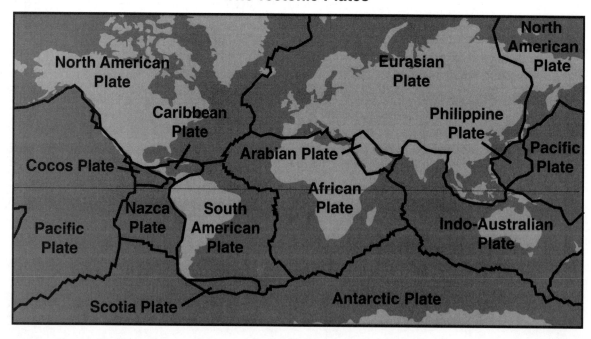

Student Inquiry Activity 9 : Sandy Shores

Topic: Sand

Introductory Statement:

Everyone enjoys a nice day at the beach. In these activities, you will carefully observe sand and speculate about how it is formed, transported, and deposited.

> **NSES Content Standard D: Structure of the Earth System**
> Landforms are the result of a combination of constructive and destructive forces. Constructive forces include crustal deformation, volcanic eruption, and deposition of sediment, while destructive forces include weathering and erosion.

Science Skills and Concepts:

- Students will infer processes that shape sand and its location.
- Students will identify conditions that result in various types of sand.
- Students will associate sand with water.

Materials/Safety Concerns:

Silica sand
Regular coarse-grained sand
Sifting sieves of varying degrees
Hand lenses
Probes
Tweezers
Small condiment cups
Paper plates

Content Background:

Students may not initially consider sand to be rocks and minerals; however, this indeed is the case. **Sand** consists of small rock and mineral particles ranging in size from 0.06 to 2 mm in diameter. Students will readily associate sand with beaches and shorelines, a common experience for many. Sand is transported to beaches by the movement of water and wave energy. Beaches are formed where water moves more sand particles toward the beach than away from it. Beaches are representative of the rocks native to an area. Students will likely be familiar with sands made from granite because of the prevalence of this type of rock in North America. On the other hand, the black sand beaches of Hawaii are formed from volcanic rock native to the island.

Rivers are another common source of shoreline sand. As with beaches, sand is transported by water and deposited along the shore. Sand from rivers typically originates from rocks and minerals within the river valley.

Student Inquiry Activity 9: Sandy Shores (cont.)

Procedures:

1. Distribute an equal volume of regular, coarse-grained sand to each pair of students. Challenge students to determine what sand is made of. Ask for creative ways to determine the composition of sand, e.g., is it small rocks? small minerals? both?

2. Urge students to devise ways to sort the sand particles for identification.

3. Instruct students to separate the sand into small cups for positive identification. Provide field guides and reference materials for identification of samples. Urge students to recall information learned from the identification of rocks and minerals.

4. To the extent possible, order the cups from most prevalent to least prevalent. Aggregate data to check for consistency across groups.

5. Repeat steps 1–4 with an equal volume of silica sand (do not tell them the name of the sand). Compare the findings to those of coarse-grained sand. Allow students to render explanations of why the sand is different, e.g., under what condition does it occur?

6. Assign students to compile a list of rocks of which sand is a key ingredient. Provide field guides and reference materials for clues. Encourage students to identify commonalities within these types of rocks, e.g., focus on the role of water transportation of sand particles to locations in which sand-bearing rocks are formed.

Name: _____   Date: _____

Student Inquiry Activity 9 : Sandy Shores (cont.)

Exploration/Data Collection:

1. Do you believe that sand is rocks, minerals, or both? Explain your reasoning.

   _____

   _____

   _____

   _____

2. Examine your cup of sand carefully and record your observations. You may pour the sand onto the paper plate, but be careful not to spill any.

   _____

   _____

   _____

3. Devise a plan to separate the sand into groups that only contain the same types of particles. Outline your plan below, and then try it!

   _____

   _____

   _____

   _____

4. Separate the sand into the small condiment cups. Only include the same types of particles in each cup.

5. To the best of your ability, identify the particles in each cup, and create a label for each cup. Also, list the different types of particles below. You may need to use field guides and reference materials to refresh your memory!

   _____

   _____

   _____

Student Inquiry Activity 9 : Sandy Shores (cont.)

6. Arrange the small cups in order from the most to least (amount). Record your data below. Be prepared to share your data with the class.

_____

_____

_____

7. Repeat the above steps for a second cup of sand that will be provided by your instructor.

_____

_____

_____

_____

_____

_____

_____

_____

8. Compare and contrast the two types of sand. Record similarities and differences.

_____

_____

_____

_____

9. In what ways do you think sand is transported? Why?

_____

_____

_____

_____

Name: _____ Date: _____

Student Inquiry Activity 9 : Sandy Shores (cont.)

10. In what ways do you think sand is deposited? Explain.

_____

_____

_____

_____

_____

11. Why do you think most of the grains are round?

_____

_____

_____

_____

_____

12. Compile a list of rocks of which sand is a key ingredient. Utilize field guides and reference materials for clues. Identify commonalities with these types of rocks. Record your observations below.

_____

_____

_____

_____

_____

13. Return to Question #1. Would you like to change your response? Why or why not?

_____

_____

_____

_____

_____

Name: _____ Date: _____

Student Inquiry Activity 9 : Sandy Shores (cont.)

Summary/What to Look For:

1. To what extent did students accurately infer processes that shape sand and its location?
2. To what extent did students accurately identify conditions that result in various types of sand?
3. To what extent did students accurately associate sand with water?

Extension and Real-World Applications:

1. Investigate the relationship between sand beaches and tides.

Discussion Questions/Assessment:

1. On your Earth model, add large areas of sand where they are currently located in the world. Insert toothpick flags to clarify your intended information. Be sure to explain how you think the sand got to these areas.

2. On your Earth model, identify the type of sand that would likely be found on beaches in your state. Cross-reference the poster to include a description of why the sand is of this nature. Insert a toothpick flag that labels this type of sand.

3. On your poster, demonstrate understanding of the importance of water in transporting sand.

4. Return to the K-W-L chart. Examine the columns for additions and editing needs based upon what you have learned during these activities, e.g., in what ways has your thinking changed?

Student Inquiry Activity **10** : Lasting Impressions

Topic: Fossils

Introductory Statement:
Fossils contain clues to the past. We can learn about plants and animals from many years ago by carefully examining fossils. In these activities, you will discover how fossils were formed; you will also make some more modern fossils.

NSES Content Standard D: Structure of the Earth System
Living organisms have played many roles in the earth system, including affecting the composition of the atmosphere, producing some types of rocks, and contributing to the weathering of rocks.
Landforms are the result of a combination of constructive and destructive forces. Constructive forces include crustal deformation, volcanic eruption, and deposition of sediment, while destructive forces include weathering and erosion.

Science Skills and Concepts:
• Students will infer fossils as clues to past plant and animal life.
• Students will create model molds of modern fossils.
• Students will analyze local fossils for clues to living conditions in the past.

Materials/Safety Concerns:

Leaves, twigs, shells, bark
Modeling clay
Samples of fossils
Plaster of Paris
Petroleum jelly
Large rubber bands

1-inch dowel rods
Waxed paper
Samples of fossils found locally
Shallow pan
Dry chicken thigh or leg bone
Liquid latex

Content Background:
Fossils can be formed in several ways. Occasionally, **entire organisms** are preserved in some type of material. Insects are sometimes preserved in resins from trees, which eventually become amber. Giant woolly mammoths have been discovered in the frozen tundra of the north. More typical are fossil remains of the hard parts of animals, e.g., bones, teeth. Students' common frame of reference for such fossils might be popular dinosaur digs on the North American continent.

It is important to differentiate between fossil molds and casts. **Mold fossils** are the impressions left by plants and animals in a rock after the plants or animals have decayed. **Cast fossils** are formed by minerals that have collected in the mold of what was once a plant or animal. As the plant or animal decays bit by bit, minerals replace what was the plant or animal, forming a cast or model.

Fossils provide clues to the types of plants and animals that were present many years ago. Fossils are important clues in determining the order in which layers of rocks were formed. Such fossils are called **index fossils**.

Student Inquiry Activity 10 : Lasting Impressions (cont.)

Procedures:

1. Ask students to record a definition for fossils and how they were formed. Allow students to share their current understanding of fossils.

2. Briefly explain the difference between fossil casts and molds. Indicate that students will work in pairs to create their own modern-day version of each.

3. Form groups of two students. Distribute needed materials for fossil molds. Allow students to collect objects of which they would like to make imprints. For the purposes of this activity, relatively flat items with distinctive features work best, e.g., fresh leaves, fern fronds, bark, shells, coins, keys, etc.

4. Guide students as they make imprints of the objects. Using a dowel rod, roll out a thin layer of modeling clay. Place the item to be imprinted directly on the clay. Place a sheet of waxed paper over the object and gently re-roll over the top of the object. Carefully remove the waxed paper and object. An imprint (thin mold) of the object should remain.

5. Lead a class discussion of how this activity is analogous to the creation of real fossils. Explain that if it were a real fossil, most of the object would have decayed and become chemically replaced by minerals.

6. Ask students how they think scientists could use fossils as clues to the past. Stress the importance of the types of rocks in which certain fossils are found, e.g., ask students to infer what information fossils may provide about the environmental conditions of that particular time.

7. Provide a variety of fossils for students to observe. Encourage students to bring in samples that they have found. Provide reference materials and field guides to assist with identification.

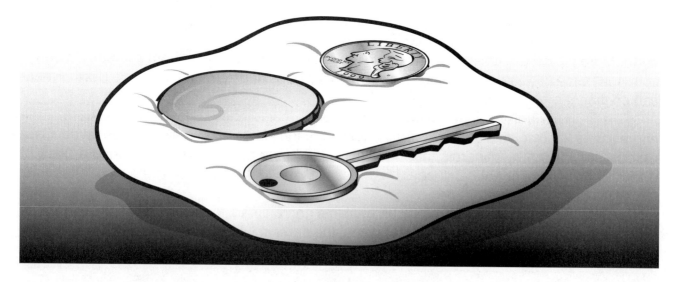

Name: _____ Date: _____

Student Inquiry Activity 10 : Lasting Impressions (cont.)

Exploration/Data Collection:

1. In your own words, write what you believe to be the definition of a fossil.

   _____

   _____

   _____

   _____

2. Provide examples of fossils and briefly explain how you think they are formed.

   _____

   _____

   _____

   _____

   _____

   _____

Lasting Impressions

1. Collect a variety of flat, thin objects, such as fresh leaves, shells, fern fronds, keys, coins, etc. Create a list of the materials you have collected below.

   _____

   _____

   _____

2. Using a dowel rod, roll out a thin layer of modeling clay. Place an object directly on the clay; cover the object with a sheet of waxed paper. Gently roll the dowel rod back and forth across the object. Carefully remove the waxed paper, and gently lift out the object. Observe what remains. Repeat with other objects.

3. Draw what you see after removing the waxed paper and the object.

Name: _____ Date: _____

Student Inquiry Activity 10 : Lasting Impressions (cont.)

4. In what ways is this similar to fossils?

_____

_____

_____

_____

5. In what ways might scientists use fossils as clues to the past?

_____

_____

_____

_____

6. Using reference materials and field guides, practice identifying the fossils supplied by your teacher. Pay particular attention to the types of rock in which the fossils were found. Draw and label several fossils below.

7. Research to find what types of fossils would most likely be found in your community, region, and state. What clues do these fossils provide about living conditions many years ago?

_____

_____

_____

_____

_____

Name: _____ Date: _____

Student Inquiry Activity 10 : Lasting Impressions (cont.)

Summary/What to Look For:
1. To what extent did students accurately infer fossils as clues to past plant and animal life?
2. To what extent did students accurately create models of modern fossils?
3. To what extent did students accurately analyze locally found fossils for clues to living conditions in the past?

Extension and Real-World Applications:
1. Fossil casts can be made using plaster of Paris; adult supervision is recommended.
   a. Mix plaster of Paris to the consistency of pancake batter.
   b. Pour a thin layer into a small, shallow pan.
   c. Coat an object, e.g., chicken bone, with vegetable oil or a thin layer of petroleum jelly; insert the object into the plaster of Paris, and allow it to dry.
   d. Coat the entire surface with a thin layer of petroleum jelly, including the bone.
   e. Pour another layer of plaster of Paris over the top.
   f. When the model is dry, split it apart at the seam and remove the bone.
   g. On one half of the plaster, bore a thin channel from the edge to the impression left by the bone.
   h. Reattach both halves of the plaster of Paris and secure them tightly with large rubber bands.
   i. Pour liquid latex into the channel until the hole left by the bone is full. Allow to dry completely.
   j. Reopen the halves, and discover the cast of the bone.

2. If possible, incorporate a field trip to a fossil-rich environment. Perhaps this could be done in conjunction with a field trip to a road-cut while studying sedimentary rocks as well. An expert on fossils would be a great addition to the trip!

Discussion Questions/Assessment:
1. On your Earth model, insert toothpick flags in or near your state with information about the types of fossils found locally. Cross-reference the information to your poster, where drawings and labels of these fossils can be added.

2. Return to the K-W-L chart. Examine the columns for additions and editing needs based upon what you have learned during these activities, e.g., in what ways has your thinking changed?

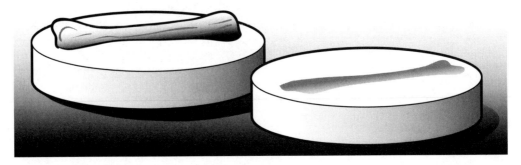

Student Inquiry Activity **11** : Independent Investigation

Topic: Student Inquiry

Introductory Statement:

In this activity, you will identify a question you have about rocks and minerals, create a plan to answer the question, find the answer(s) to your question, draw conclusions based on the answer(s) to your question, report your findings to others, and identify new questions that emerged as you looked for the answer(s) to the question.

NSES Content Standard A: Understanding About Scientific Inquiry

The following are indicators that suggest students meet NSES Content Standard A: Understanding About Scientific Inquiry:

- "Different kinds of questions suggest different kinds of scientific investigations. Some investigations involve observing and describing objects, organisms, or events; some involve collecting specimens; some involve experiments; some involve seeking more information; some involve discovery of new objects and phenomena; and some involve making models.

- Current scientific knowledge and understanding guide scientific investigations. Different scientific domains employ different methods, core theories, and standards to advance scientific knowledge and understanding.

- Technology is used to gather data accurately and allows scientists to analyze and quantify the results of investigations.

- Scientific explanations emphasize evidence, have logically consistent arguments, and use scientific principles, models, and theories. The scientific community accepts and uses such explanations until displaced by better scientific ones. When such displacement occurs, science advances.

- Science advances through legitimate skepticism. Asking questions and querying other scientists' explanations is part of scientific inquiry. Scientists evaluate the explanations proposed by other scientists by examining evidence, comparing evidence, identifying faulty reasoning, pointing out statements that go beyond evidence, and suggesting alternative explanations for the same observations.

- Scientific investigations sometimes result in new ideas and phenomena for study, generate new methods or procedures for an investigation, or develop new technologies to improve the collection of data. All of these results can lead to new investigations." (p. 118, NRC, 1996)

Student Inquiry Activity **11** : Independent Investigation (cont.)

Science Skills and Concepts:
- Students will generate a question(s) for research.
- Students will identify ways in which to seek answers to the question(s).
- Students will collect data relevant to the question(s).
- Students will analyze the data relevant to the question(s).
- Students will draw conclusions based on analysis of data.
- Students will report the results of the investigation.

Content Background:
See information contained in inquiry standards description.

Procedures:

1. Review and explain what it means to approach science from an inquiry point of view. Remind students of how this was done during one or more learning episodes from the rocks and minerals activities. Point out that in those lessons, the assigned tasks were more specified. Alert students that in this activity they will have the choice of what to investigate and how to investigate it.

   Encourage students to generate questions* they have about rocks and minerals, perhaps as a result of one or more of the activities previously completed. Refer students to the K-W-L chart to which information and new questions were added throughout the activities. Perhaps a question arose as a result of one or more activities, and time didn't allow for adequate follow-up. Perhaps new information was added to the chart, but the students may have an interest in going further, learning more. Assist them with narrowing the focus of the question(s); help them with determining questions that are manageable with available resources. Depending upon the scope and depth of the question(s), students may work individually, in pairs, or in small groups. Require students to develop a "plan of study" to be approved by the teacher.

2. As students consider questions of interest, encourage them to consider the following issues:
   - In what ways could I/we find the answer(s)?
   - What types of resources are needed to proceed with the study?
   - Is it possible to design an experiment and collect data?

3. Facilitate student investigations by providing guidance as needed. As the investigations unfold, it may become necessary to help students to reshape the questions; however, encourage students to maintain a focus on what it is they want to know. Guide students as data is collected; check for validity and reliability. Help students with ideas to locate needed resources to conduct investigations.

Student Inquiry Activity **11** : Independent Investigation (cont.)

4. Assist students with formatting data collected to enhance analysis. Suggest a guiding question such as "What does this data mean?" The key is to interpret the data so that conclusions can be drawn. Students should carefully consider how to present the data, along with conclusions drawn and questions for further research.

5. Share the investigations with others. Suggested formats may include a mini-science conference, a science fair, displays, in-class presentations, etc.

* Some sample topics may include:
- How do minerals compare with the types of minerals commonly associated with vitamins?
- Why are minerals found in certain locations of the earth and not others?
- What are the most common rocks and minerals around our area? Why are they found here?
- What causes the various colors of rocks and minerals?
- What are gems, and how do they compare to rocks and minerals? What makes a gem, a gem?
- What causes plate tectonics, and in what direction is the North American plate moving?
- What are various types of volcanoes, and what are the differences between them?
- How are mining operations run?
- What are some programs designed to protect the land from the ill effects of mining?
- What steps must I take to begin a rocks, minerals, and/or fossils collection?
- What do geologists do? What training is required?

Summary/What to Look For:
1. To what extent did students accurately generate a question(s) for research?
2. To what extent did students accurately identify ways in which to seek answers to the question(s)?
3. To what extent did students accurately collect data relevant to the question(s)?
4. To what extent did students accurately analyze the data relevant to the question(s)?
5. To what extent did students accurately draw conclusions based on analysis of data?
6. To what extent did students accurately report the results of the investigation?
7. To what extent did students accurately generate new questions as a result of the investigation?

Extension Ideas and Interdisciplinary Applications

Rocks and Geography:

1. Use reference materials to identify and map the underlying types of rocks in your county, state, and region. Focus on the prominent landforms of these areas; what forces were responsible for these, e.g., glaciers, mountain uplifting, volcanism, etc.?

Rocks and Minerals Pen Pals:

1. Establish a pen-pal relationship with a class from another region of the United States. Challenge them to exchange information related to the rocks and landforms of their region. Create a videotape that contains a challenge question related to rocks and minerals. Send the videotape to the pen-pal class for a response. The pen-pal class should research/problem-solve and return their findings along with a new challenge for your class. The video can be sent back and forth throughout the year.

Grow Your Own Crystals:

To supplement the study of minerals, an extended investigation of crystal formation is recommended. Crystal kits can be obtained from any major science supply catalog and/or at hobby shops. For those who are on a more limited budget, crystals can be grown using basic materials found in most kitchens. Both recipes appear in *Spencer Christian's World of Wonders: Is There a Dinosaur in Your Backyard?* by Spencer Christian and Antonia Felix (see reference list for complete bibliographic information). Adult supervision is required for both activities.

1. Sugar Crystals

   Add 1.5 cups of sugar to one-half cup of water; boil and place in a clear container, e.g, Pyrex™ measuring container. Tie a piece of heavy string to a pencil. Suspend the string into the saturated sugar solution, e.g., lay the pencil across the top of the container. Observe what happens over a period of one week. Assuming all containers/materials were clean, these crystals would be edible. Try the same procedure, substituting with salt. Compare and contrast the results.

2. Crystal Garden

   Place four to five medium-sized rocks and several charcoal briquette pieces in a foil pan. Measure 3 tablespoons of salt, 3 tablespoons of water, and 3 tablespoons of liquid laundry bluing; mix together and carefully add 1 tablespoon of ammonia. Caution: keep ammonia away from eyes, mouth, and nose; follow safety precautions as per label instructions. Spoon the mixed solution onto the charcoal pieces and rocks; do not allow excess solution to create a pool in the bottom of the pan. Observe the set-up for a period of two to three days. Research to determine what has happened and how this is related to crystal formation within magmas. **Safety goggles are recommended for this activity.**

Extension Ideas and Interdisciplinary Applications (cont.)

Rocks, Minerals, and Fossils Collecting:

Rocks, minerals, and fossils collecting can turn into a lifetime hobby. What better time to expose students to the basic materials, safety precautions, and procedures of rocks, minerals, and fossils collecting?

1. Begin by building a rocks, minerals, and fossils collection kit. Recommended items include a rock hammer, awl/strong probe, chisel, hand lens, field guide, compass, geologic maps, storage bags, field journal, safety glasses/goggles, hard hat, pocket knife, small bottle of vinegar, porcelain streak plate, glass plate, coins, tissue for wrapping specimens, and a small brush. These items would fit nicely into a backpack.

2. Determine ideal locations for collection within your area, e.g., quarries, exposed beds and/or outcroppings, remnants of flood cuts, etc. Information from the state geological survey will be valuable in locating these areas in your region. Learn and obey safety rules and regulations of local sites. Take copious field notes as samples are collected; this should include location, description of the parent rock formation and surrounding environment, sketches, and observations. Avoid indiscriminate hammering in the collection of samples; only hammer as needed to dislodge a sample.

3. Upon return to the lab/classroom, the samples will likely need to be cleaned. A soft brush works well for most rocks; however, some minerals are friable and will easily be damaged. Distilled water is recommended for cleaning rocks; of course, some crystals will dissolve if exposed to water, e.g., halite. Alcohol cleans sulfates; a weak hydrochloric acid solution cleans silicates.

4. All samples should be identified to the best of your ability. Beginning rock collectors may wish to use phrases such as "this is a granite-like rock." Consider how you wish to display samples. Small boxes lined with tissue are good for long-term storage. If possible, store the small boxes in pullout drawers for easy access and viewing. Some people prefer to mount and display samples in glass-covered boxes; although this is more expensive, it affords one the opportunity to transport the collection.

5. In all cases, students should be supervised and have received parental permission to collect rocks, minerals, and fossils. For students with an avid interest in this hobby, after-school and summer collecting field trips would be wonderful opportunities. Students will likely enjoy sharing their findings with others, e.g., students, administrators, parents. Rocks, minerals, and fossils collecting can result in community-involvement opportunities, e.g., perhaps students could share their findings at the local nursing home; perhaps students could coordinate a community rocks and minerals show.

Student Literature Resources

Barrow, Lloyd H. *Adventures with Rocks and Minerals.* Enslow Publishers, Inc.
    ISBN 0-89490-624-0

Beattie, Lauras. *Discover Rocks and Minerals.* Creative Company. ISBN 0-911239-36-7

Chesterman, Charles. *National Audubon Society Field Guide to North American Rocks and Minerals.* Alfred A. Knopf. ISBN 0-394-50269-8

Christian, Spencer and Felix, Antonia. *Is There a Dinosaur in Your Backyard?* John Wiley & Sons, Inc. ISBN 0-471-19616-9

Comfort, Iris Tracy. *Earth Treasures: Rocks and Minerals.* Prentice-Hall, Inc.

Downs, Sandra. *Earth's Hidden Treasures.* Twenty-first Century Books. ISBN 0-7613-1411-3

Fuller, Sue. *Rocks and Minerals.* Dorling Kindersley, Inc. ISBN 1-56458-663-4

Horenstein, Sidney. *Rocks Tell Stories.* The Millbrook Press. ISBN 1-56294-238-7

Jennings, Terry. *Rocks and Soil.* Children's Press. ISBN 0-516-48407-9

Kittinger, Jo S. *A Look at Rocks from Coal to Kimberlite.* Franklin Watts, Inc.
    ISBN 0-531-20310-7

Lambert, David. *Rocks and Minerals.* Franklin Watts, Inc. ISBN 0-531-10165-7

Olifee, Neesha, Olifee, Jon, and Raham, Gary. *The Deep Time Diaries.* Fulcrum Publishing.
    ISBN 1-55591-415-2

Parker, Steve. *Rocks and Minerals.* Dorling Kindersley, Inc. ISBN 1-56458-394-5

Pellant, Helen. *Rocks and Minerals.* Dorling Kindersley, Inc. ISBN 1-56458-033-4

Pough, Frederic H. *Rocks and Minerals.* Houghton Mifflin Company. ISBN 0-395-91097-8

Rhodes, Frank H. T. *Geology.* Golden Press.

Ritter, Rhoda. *Rocks and Fossils.* Franklin Watts, Inc. ISBN 0-531-00358-2

Rydell, Wendy. *Discovering Fossils.* Troll Associates. ISBN 0-89375-974-0

Symes, R. F. *Rocks and Minerals.* Dorling Kindersley, Inc. ISBN 0-7894-6551-5

Symes, R. F. and Harding R. R. *Crystal and Gem.* Dorling Kindersley, Inc.
    ISBN 0-7894-6574-4

Williams, Brian. *Mining.* Raintree Steck Vaughn Publishers. ISBN 0-8114-4789-8

Curriculum Resources

Illinois State Geological Survey,
GeoActivities Series
Department of Natural Resources
Natural Resources Building
615 East Peabody Dr.
Champaign, IL 61820

DSM II Earth Science: Rocks and Minerals,
Grades 5–6
*Delta Science Module
http://www.delta-education.com
*see also Erosion

Science & Technology for Children: Rocks and Minerals, Grade 3
National Science Resources Center
ISBN 0-89278-746-5
Carolina Biological Supply
2700 York Road
Burlington, NC 27215
800-334-5551
http://www.carolina.com/

Plate Tectonics, The Way the Earth Works,
Grades 6–8
Great Explorations in Mathematics and Science
(GEMS)
ISBN 0-924886-60-9
Lawrence Hall of Science
University of California
Berkeley, CA 94720
http://www.lhs.berkeley.edu/gems/

Stories in Stone, Grades 4–9
Great Explorations in Mathematics and Science
(GEMS)
ISBN 0-912511-93-1
Lawrence Hall of Science
University of California
Berkeley, CA 94720
http://www.lhs.berkeley.edu/gems/

Down to Earth, Grades 5–9
Activities Integrating Mathematics and Science
(AIMS)
ISBN 1-881431-00-2
AIMS Education Foundation
P.O. Box 8120
Fresno, CA 93747-8120
209-255-4094
http://www.aimsedu.org/

Project Earth Science: Geology, Grades 5–8
by Brent A. Ford
ISBN 0-87355-131-1
National Science Teachers Association
1840 Wilson Boulevard
Arlington, VA 22201-3000
www.nsta.org

Rocks & Minerals, Grades 7–12
by Doris Metcalf and Ron Marson
Task Oriented Physical Science (TOPS)
10970 S. Mulina Rd.
Canby, OH 97013
http://www.topscience.org/

Classroom Resources

Ward's Natural Science
5100 W. Henrietta Rd.
P.O. Box 92912
Rochester, NY 14692-9012
www.wardsci.com

Frey Scientific
905 Hickory Lane
P.O. Box 8101
Mansfield, OH 44901-8101
800-225-FREY (3739)
www.freyscientific.com

Recommended Websites

http://www.usgs.gov/ (highly recommended; see education link)

http://www.mii.org/

http://www.rocksforkids.com/

http://www.nearctica.com/family/kids/krocks.htm

http://www.fi.edu/fellows/payton/rocks/index2.html

http://RockhoundingAR.com/pebblepups.html

State Geological Survey: Conduct a web search (e.g., Yahoo) for your state geological survey, e.g., "Iowa State Geological Survey."

References

Chesterman, C., and Lowe, K. (1979). *National Audubon Society Field Guide to North American Rocks and Minerals.* New York, NY: Alfred A. Knopf.

Christian, S., and Felix, A. (1998). *Is There a Dinosaur in Your Backyard?* New York, NY: John Wiley & Sons, Inc.

Cvancara, A. (1985). *A Field Manual for the Amateur Geologist.* New York, NY: John Wiley & Sons, Inc.

Dixon, D. and Bernor, R. (1992). *The Practical Geologist.* New York, NY: Simon & Schuster/ Fireside.

Ford, B. (1996). *Project Earth Science: Geology.* Arlington, VA: National Science Teachers Association.

Fuller, S. (1995). *Rocks and Minerals.* New York, NY: Dorling Kindersley, Inc.

National Research Council. (1996). *National Science Education Standards.* Washington, D.C.: National Academy Press.

Pellant, C. (1992). *Rocks and Minerals.* New York, NY: Dorling Kindersley, Inc.

Pough, F. (1953). *A Field Guide to Rocks and Minerals.* Boston, MA: Houghton Mifflin Company.

Sager, R., Ramsey, W., Phillips, C., and Watenpaugh, F. (2002). *Modern Earth Science.* Austin, TX: Holt, Rinehart & Winston.

Tarbuck, E., and Lutgens, F. (1997). *Earth Science.* Upper Saddle River, NJ: Prentice-Hall.